T0374274

Every once in awhile I meet someone that I wish I could get to know better. Only to find that when I did get to know them, the closer I got, the more disappointed I became. When it comes to my friend Jim Butcher the opposite is the case. The closer I got the better he looked, which was a blessing to me. I always want to be around people whose character is magnetic. People, who when I am with them, make me want a bit of them to rub off on me. Jim is one of those people and I trust that as you read this interesting reflection on a life well lived that something of Jim will rub off on you as well.

Jim writes of his life experiences through the lens of his rearview mirror. As he reflects from a few years north of the eighty mark, he shares a unique perspective on life that no doubt he wouldn't have been able to articulate if he had written this in the earlier years of his life. Looking back near the end of the journey clarifies our values; our mistakes are seen through the filter of what we have learned, and things that we thought were so very important then are now seen as far less significant. This makes the 'life in the long view' perspective from Jim both inspiring and instructive.

I met Jim when I became his pastor in Kokomo, Indiana. I was young in the ministry and he was well into his career as a distinguished lawyer. Aside from the fact that he fell asleep during my sermon when visiting my previous church as a member of the search committee from Kokomo 😊, I found him to be a delightfully engaging person who was always interested in the well being of his pastor. He quickly became more than a parishioner. He became my friend. And I treasure the fond memories of our friendship. Every pastor should be so blessed to have someone like Jim by his side.

Kokomo is a relatively small community where news about its leading citizens passes rapidly through the neighborhoods. Interestingly, news about Jim was never the negative kind that people love to share. His helping hand as an attorney was well known and his dealings with others were above reproach. Which is why he won by a landslide when the time came for him to be our region's representative in the Indiana State Senate. To the glory of God, Jim was unashamedly known as a follower of Jesus and people could easily connect the dots as to why Jim was the kind of man that he is.

In this reveal of the journey of his life you will sense the heartbeat of a person who has a passion to serve Christ and others. From his early days of giving up a lucrative job as a civil servant to serve young people nationally, to generously using his gifts as an attorney to bless others as well as serving the best interests of Kokomo citizens as a State Senator, Jim was a tireless benefactor to the flourishing of others and the best interests of his community. And he was and is a dedicated churchman. Now, decades after my brief stint as his pastor, he remains a loyal and enthusiastic participant in the ministry of Bible Baptist Church.

But most importantly, in the midst of the busyness of his highly engaged life, he and his equally dedicated wife Marvel were committed to prioritize their love for each other and their family. In fact, Jim has written this book for his grandchildren to read as an inspiration for them to carry the torch forward as people of character and competency who live for the good of others and the glory of God...just like their grandpa.

Thanks, Jim, for letting us have a peek into what you have shared with your grandkids. We are the better for reading it!

Joe Stowell
Pastor and Friend

I'm glad Jim Butcher took the time to write his autobiography. Readers will now have the opportunity to read about a unique person who has had an impact on countless individuals because of his love for the Lord Jesus Christ and his love for America and our heritage, especially President Abraham Lincoln. This twofold love fueled his desire to make a difference in the lives of those around him through his involvement in the political arena, his role as an attorney and as a leader in his community and Indiana.

You will learn about his humble upbringing and the lessons he was taught that helped to mold his character at an early age; and which have been passed down to his children, his grandchildren and his great grandchildren.

I first met Jim after his election to the Indiana State Senate in 1978. During his eight years in the General Assembly, Jim was known as a leader on issues impacting the families of Indiana. He was uncompromising when it came to dealing with an issue that dealt with Biblical values. Jim was respected by his Senate colleagues in both political parties.

Jim was instrumental in the founding of Citizens Concerned for the Constitution in November, 1980. Jim's advice, counsel, support and encouragement over the years has helped CCC, now known as Advance America, to grow from a handful of citizens in 1980 to now being the largest pro-family and pro-church organization in Indiana.

No Regrets, will be an encouragement to everyone who desires to live a life dedicated to following Jesus Christ and who wants to serve others as they travel the road of life the Lord has for them.

Eric I. Miller
Attorney at Law
Founder, Advance America, Inc.

My 41-years of employment with Jim Butcher began in March, 1978. I was 8 months pregnant. He hired me as his office manager, and we agreed I would work two days a week. My daughter, Keri Ann, was born April 6, 1978, and I discovered the joy and love of becoming a mother. I quickly realized that motherhood and working (even two days a week) were challenging and told Jim Butcher I regretted that I would have to leave his employment.

He quickly asked me why. I responded that I needed to be at home with my daughter and could not be at the office eight hours. He said, "I will make you a deal. Work four hours on Monday, four hours on Friday, take work home; he further stated, I will never ask you to put this job ahead of God or your family." He was truly a man ahead of his time by offering job flexibility and working from home. I accepted his offer, and we both found this arrangement to work well.

Jim Butcher kept his word for 41 years. Through those years, I had the joy of the birth of my second daughter, Linda, experienced the death of my first husband, Kerry, met and married my husband, Jim Buck, and had the miracle of our third daughter, Laura. Throughout these years and life experiences, Jim Butcher kept his word: God first, family second, job third. He allowed me to flex my job responsibilities around my family responsibilities. This was a gift for which I will always be grateful.

Jim Butcher and I knew how to wear many hats and knew how to take one off and put on another. We wore the hat of the office finances; we wore the hat of politics for which we both shared a passion, interest and involvement; we wore the hat of our faith in Jesus Christ and shared much through the years of what He was doing and had done in our lives; and we wore the hat of friendship.

When I became a part of the law firm, I also had the added benefit of becoming friends with Marvel Butcher. She has been such a blessing in my life and has helped me through many challenging times in my life's journey.

I am so thankful my life path crossed with the life paths of Jim Butcher and Marvel Butcher and that the Lord brought us together to work together and to be friends. I love them both so very much.

Judy Buck
Law Office Manager and Friend

I have known Jim Butcher for 55 years. He and his wife, Marvel, moved to Kokomo where he worked as the Planning Director for the Kokomo and Howard County planning commissions and later opened his law office. I have watched his passion for the gospel as he used his unique skills to minister to people from all walks of life. Join him as he shares his journey of his faithfulness to God and God's faithfulness to Jim and his family.

Jerry Fiscus
Friend

William Shakespeare once wrote that "all the world is a stage and we all must play our part." If that is true, James R. Butcher has played his part writ large. Well known and respected as a community leader, attorney, elected official, Christian stalwart and family man, Jim Butcher has certainly made this mark and significant impressions on all of those blessed to have made his acquaintance or have interacted with him.

I've personally known Jim Butcher for over fifty years. I first met Jim in his role as a father to Kevin, one of my high school football teammates. When I returned to Kokomo after college and my first employment, Jim was one of the first people to greet me. Although there was a generational age difference, I knew that Jim and I would be friends and associates in the coming years.

When Jim decided to run for Congress in 1986, he asked me to be his campaign finance chairman. It was a pleasure working in this capacity. Normally, raising political funds is somewhat akin to oral surgery. With candidate Jim Butcher, all I had to do was ask for help. The people who knew Jim stepped forward with their checkbooks in hand. During the campaign I suggested to Jim that we might raise some additional funds from the "party" wing of the Grand Old Party if we had cash bars at our fund-raising receptions. I was a little disappointed when Jim told me that he had never had to have alcohol at any of his political events and he didn't want to start now. I thought he was wrong, but I was the one who was wrong. I appreciated Jim's resistance to compromising his values in the quest for public office. It was a character trait of his that I greatly admired.

In 1985, Jim Butcher did the legal work for the adoption of our son, Jeremy. The process of adoption required both birth parents to sign documents terminating their parental rights. The birth mother signed the paperwork without hesitation. The birth father balked at signing the documents. After considerable persuasion by Jim Butcher to do the right thing, the birth father finally relented and signed the necessary consent and the adoption was finalized. I don't remember ever receiving a bill for Jim's services.

No Regrets is a humble and frank examination of Jim Butcher's life in his own words. It is amazing to think that such an extraordinary life can be summed up in so few pages, but that is the gist of Jim Butcher, long on action but lacking bravado and self-promotion. My father used to like to say that "lives of all great men remind, what we can live our lives sublime." I'd like to think that he was talking about Jim Butcher, a man who has touched the lives and hearts of our community and made our country a better place to live.

Craig Dunn
Financial Advisor and Friend

"This is a must read about a life well lived. Jim shares how living life with God at the center has blessed him in many ways. You will be drawn into Jim's journey from humble beginning to a wonderful marriage, incredible children and a career filled with excitement, passion and opportunities to make a difference in the communities he lived. Along the way Jim illustrates how life sometimes has unexpected twists and turns and takes you in directions you were not expecting. Through the surprises you will be inspired by the grace in which Jim handled adversity and the triumphs that led to greater things. This is a must read for those who wish to be a better husband, father, neighbor and friend and to understand how God may just have a plan for you.

This is a feel good story in these times of uncertainty."

Paul Wyman
Realtor, County Commissioner and Neighbor

NO REGRETS

JAMES R. BUTCHER

WESTBOW
PRESS®
A DIVISION OF THOMAS NELSON
& ZONDERVAN

WestBow Press books may be ordered through booksellers or by contacting:

WestBow Press
A Division of Thomas Nelson & Zondervan
1663 Liberty Drive
Bloomington, IN 47403
www.westbowpress.com
844-714-3454

Scripture taken from the New King James Version® Copyright © 1982 by Thomas Nelson. Used by permission. All rights reserved.

ISBN: 978-1-6642-6633-9 (sc)
ISBN: 978-1-6642-6632-2 (e)

Library of Congress Control Number: 2022908564

Print information available on the last page.

WestBow Press rev. date: 05/19/2022

We would have been married for 69 years on
June 27, 2022. This book is dedicated to my wonderful
wife for all the blessings she showered upon me and
upon our family. Her legacy and Christian faith
live on in the lives of her many family members and
myriad of friends; she will never be forgotten.

CONTENTS

CHAPTER 1

"Humble Beginnings"

My parents, James Otis Butcher and Beulah Iris Gammon were born in rural eastern Tennessee in the early 1900's. Dad was born in 1906 and mother was born in 1904. They were married in Union County, Tennessee on September 1, 1923 by a justice of the peace. Both of my parents came from large families and had to leave school early in life to work in the cotton and tobacco fields to help support their parents and many siblings. Dad left school in the 10th grade and Mother dropped out of school in the 8th grade.

My folks moved to Detroit, Michigan in the late 1920's to find employment. My dad found work in the food business and told me he had actually unloaded box-cars of bananas with the infamous Jimmy Hoffa.

Dad was a man who stood about five feet, six inches tall and weighed about 145 pounds. But he was one of the strongest men I have ever met. Dad drove a grocery truck for the C. F. Smith Grocery Company all over the city of Detroit and surrounding suburbs for many years. As I was growing up, Dad occasionally would allow me to ride along with him on his deliveries. I stood in awe as Dad would throw half a cow over his shoulder and carry it into the freezer through the back of the grocery store. Some of those slabs of meat had to weigh almost as much as Dad!

Although I was born in Detroit, Michigan at the Florence Crittenton Hospital, on March 9, 1933, my folks moved to Hazel Park, a suburb starting just north of Eight Mile Road, the northern border of Detroit city limits.

Dad subsequently got a job at the Allegheny-Ludlum Steel Company in suburban Ferndale, Michigan where he worked in the rolling mill to help forge red hot metal into huge steel bars.

My childhood was fairly unremarkable and I always felt love from both of my parents. Serving God was their number one priority and we were in church no less than three times per week.

My father sang in several gospel quartets during the 40's and 50's and was very instrumental in starting gospel singing conventions in the greater Detroit, Michigan area. His quartet sang on the radio for several years at a station in Royal Oak, Michigan. In fact, shortly after I met Marvel, my fiancée, she joined a newly formed trio and sang with my father.

At one point in my growing up years my father was gone a lot with gospel music demands, so much so that my mother had a nervous breakdown and was hospitalized for several days. Fortunately, their marriage prevailed in spite of some anxious days during this period. I was old enough to be concerned but do not feel those difficult times had any long term negative effect upon my life.

My mother was a homemaker and never worked outside of the home during her married life. Mother never learned to drive a car and was known for walking long distances everywhere she lived. Sometimes she would walk two or three miles to buy groceries or to visit friends.

My mother prayed for me every day since I was born until she passed away just shy of eighty-nine years. She felt her calling in life was to be a faithful wife to my father and a Godly mother to her son.

Any success I have ever achieved in my life; personally, athletically, or professionally, is due in large part to my mother's prayer life. I will forever be grateful to her for her devotion to God and relentless prayer for her only child.

My folks lived paycheck to paycheck all of their married lives. They never owned enough money to even open a checking or savings account during their marriage. Yet, my father was one of the most generous men I have ever known. It was well known in and around the family and the Free Will Baptist Churches in the greater Detroit area that James Otis Butcher, affectionately known by many as "Butch", would always be available if you needed money or anything else. Dad would never turn down a friend or family member if they needed twenty dollars or fifty dollars. He never kept records and he loaned much more than he was ever repaid.

My father was also a gifted Bible teacher. He started a Sunday school class which he called the JOY Bible class. Jesus first, Others second, and Yourself last. Dad lived out his life according to those values and priorities. Jesus first, others second, and yourself last.

Dad loved sports. During his early years in Detroit he played semi-pro baseball. As a boy growing up, dad would take me to the Hazel Park high school football games. At home he and I would watch the Detroit Tigers play on black and white television.

Partly because of my father's encouragement, I became involved in athletic activity from my early childhood. I remember playing softball as a 10 year old with the adult factory men's team at the ball field about a block from our home. When a team did not have nine men show up for a game, they would let this 10 year old fill in.

I literally learned to shoot a basketball at the peach basket nailed to the wall of our garage located at 1244 E. Jarvis, Hazel Park, Michigan. I remember shooting many nights by myself with the light on the back porch as my only light. Even though my parents' resources were very limited all through my growing up years, I knew if I needed a baseball glove or any other piece of athletic equipment, Dad would always come through.

In the latter part of 1970, my dad and mother came to Kokomo, Indiana to visit our family. Dad reclined on our couch for most of the visit and had a cough that he could not control. I called my local doctor, Dr. Warren McClure, who still made house calls, to come to our home on Saturday evening. Following his examination of Dad, as I walked Dr. McClure to his car, he told me to get my dad back to Detroit as soon as possible and get him to the best surgeon I could find. Dr. McClure told me that my father had lung cancer. That wasn't really too surprising since my father had smoked since he was a small boy working in the cotton and tobacco fields of Tennessee.

I took dad back to Detroit and got an appointment with a well-respected surgeon. Following his examination he confirmed that dad had late-term lung cancer. He told dad he would be wasting his time and dad's money to operate; his lungs were black as coal. Dad spent the last ninety days of his life in Bi-County Hospital in Warren, Michigan. He died quietly on January 15, 1971, at the age of sixty-four. Fortunately for Dad he did not have a lot of pain and never even asked for an aspirin.

After Dad passed away, I sold Mother's home in Hazel Park for twelve thousand dollars and moved her down to Indiana to be with us.

My beginnings in Hazel Park, Michigan were in the home of a humble Christian couple who migrated to Michigan from Tennessee. I was born into that home in 1933 during the Great Depression. In spite of the modest circumstances, my parents set the foundation for their son to dream big and have the opportunity to be successful in life beyond their expectations.

CHAPTER 2

"The Most Important Decision"

When Mom and Dad loaded their coupe automobile with all their earthly belongings and moved to Detroit, Michigan in the early 1920's, they also brought their most valuable possession, their deep faith in the Lord Jesus Christ.

When they moved to the Detroit suburban neighborhood of Hazel Park, Michigan, Dad and Mom helped to organize and establish a church named Tabernacle Baptist Church on Stephenson Highway in the heart of town. That church is still alive and functioning well today.

Not too many years later, Mom and Dad helped to form another church called First Free Will Baptist several blocks away from the tabernacle and also on Stephenson Highway. This was our church during most of my growing up years. Our family went to Sunday school, morning worship, evening worship service, and Wednesday night prayer meeting. When the church doors opened, we were there.

My father had a good tenor voice and was involved in organizing several gospel quartets during those days. For several years Dad's quartet would travel to Royal Oak, Michigan to sing gospel music on radio station WEXL. I remember sitting in an adjacent studio many nights watching and listening to the quartet spread the good news of the gospel of Jesus Christ throughout the broad listening area of lower Michigan.

Dad was also instrumental in forming "Gospel Music SINGS" at our church which ran from 2:30-4:30 P.M. on one Sunday per month. Many lives were enriched as a result.

Before Dad passed away in 1971, he helped start several other churches in the greater Detroit area. Ten Mile Free Will Baptist Church and Fifteen Mile Road Free Will Baptist Church are two of such churches. All of these churches are still viable testimonies for the cause of Christ to this very day.

Having heard many pastors and evangelists preach at our church over the years, I realized that my parents' belief in Jesus Christ was their decision. However, by the age of nine, I realized I had to make a decision about the claims of Christ found in the Bible for myself. At our church after every sermon the speaker would give an invitation to the audience to walk down the aisle and give their hearts and lives to Jesus Christ. I wanted to make that walk and give my life to the Lord, but did not have the courage to do so publicly.

On one particular Sunday night in 1942 on the way home from church I realized I could ask for forgiveness of sins and accept Jesus Christ as my Savior at any time and at any location. On that night before I went to bed, I knelt at my bed and made the most important decision of my life. I invited Jesus Christ into my life and although I did not know it at the time, secured my eternal destination.

I did not sense any great change in my life at that age, but I made a conscious choice to allow God to take control of my life and help me in all choices I would make the rest of my life.

I cannot state that I have lived the rest of my life in a manner that would always please the Lord. I have made choices over the years that I am sure displeased God. However, I can state with 100% certainty that all major decisions and choices I have made since 1942 have been made with the decision to follow God's will for my life, and with my wife and children as the primary focus. I have never been sorry for the decision to follow Jesus Christ made at nine years of age. Before I accepted Christ as my Savior, I had been thinking a lot about the length of eternity. Even at the age of nine, I decided I wanted to spend eternity with God and my family and friends.

CHAPTER 3

"Hazel Park, Michigan High School"

S ports have always been a large part of my life. When I was twelve years old, I attended twenty-five Detroit Tiger baseball games at Briggs Stadium located at the intersection of Trumbell and Michigan Avenues in downtown Detroit. Remarkably, I went to these games alone and needed to use a Detroit Street Department bus and transfer to a streetcar to arrive at the park for the games.

I normally sat in the right field bleachers and was often the only white fan in that section of the stadium. At a time in America when white and African American folks did not do a lot of activities together, I thoroughly enjoyed my fellowship with my African American brothers and sisters at the Detroit Tiger baseball games. The tickets were fifty-five cents and I obtained the money to attend the games by cashing in my soda pop bottles at five cents each.

In 1945, the Tigers won the World Series. I was such an ardent fan that I covered my bedroom walls and ceiling with the daily newspaper (Detroit Free Press) with the box scores and pictures of the games.

My family lived one block from the United Oaks Elementary School in Hazel Park which had a large playground complete with several baseball and softball diamonds, and basketball goals. I spent many summer days playing ball with my friends at the school yard.

As I entered Hazel Park High School in the fall of 1948, I wanted to play my three favorite sports, namely football, basketball, and baseball. I was blessed with a 6' 2", 165 pound body which allowed me to follow my childhood dreams. I became the first nine varsity letter winner at Hazel Park High School lettering in football, basketball, baseball, and track.

I was blessed to receive second team all Eastern Michigan league honors in both football and basketball in 1950. Our school was in a very strong league which included teams from East Detroit, Birmingham, Ferndale, Royal Oak, Mt. Clements and Port Huron; all large and well-known schools in the greater Detroit area.

I will always be indebted to my high school coaches who encouraged and instructed me to be the best I could be. A wonderful man named Dan Lutkus was my basketball coach. Ed Ripmaster, the Webster brothers and "Boz" Grba were my football coaches and Bill Zepp was my track coach. Mr. Ripmaster was also my baseball coach. I was fortunate to be voted the most outstanding senior athlete in my senior year in Hazel Park high school.

As I reflect upon my high school experience, I do have some regrets. Although I accepted Jesus Christ as my personal Savior at the age of nine, I did not exemplify my Christian faith as I should have. There were several of my classmates who belonged to the Voice of Christian Youth (VCY) Club in high school. I should have been with them as they shared their Christian faith and values on our high school campus. Unfortunately, I was not. I believe I was more interested in being a popular athlete than I was in sharing my Christian convictions with my high school classmates. As I review my 1951 Hazel Park yearbook, I am reminded of the many missed opportunities that I allowed to pass by.

I also must admit that I was more interested in girls and sports than I was in academics and good grades. I look back now and wished I had been a better, more dedicated student and Christian witness during my four year stay at Hazel Park high school.

Some of my best friends and teammates at Hazel Park high school were Doyle McIntosh, Howard Wiley, Jack Hobbs, Ray Woods, and my two cousins, Bob and Paul Clark.

CHAPTER 4

"Springfield, Ohio"

As I was approaching high school graduation from Hazel Park High School in June of 1951, I knew I wanted to continue playing sports in college. However, I had a huge problem. My folks didn't have the resources to send me, and to the best of my knowledge no one else in our immediate families (includes aunts, uncles and dozens of cousins) had ever gone to college.

Fortunately, early in the summer of 1951, I received an invitation to come to the University of Cincinnati, Ohio for a football try-out. Coaching the Cincinnati football team at that time was Syd Gilman, who later coached the San Diego Chargers professional team and if I recall correctly, also became the owner of the Chargers team before he passed away a few years ago in his mid-nineties. I caught a bus to

Cincinnati and tried out for the wide-out position on the Cincinnati University football team.

Unfortunately, Coach Gilman told me he liked my skills but I was a little "too slow" for their offense and he couldn't offer me a scholarship. When I returned back home to Hazel Park, I was contacted by Mr. Leroy Fredricks, the director of recreational activities for our community. Mr. Fredricks had followed my high school career and called me to recommend that I apply for admittance to Wittenberg College (now university) located in Springfield, Ohio. Mr. Fredricks had graduated from Wittenberg in 1935 and played football at the Lutheran school.

I contacted the college and based upon Mr. Fredricks recommendations, they offered me a partial scholarship to play football. After I accepted the offer and made plans to move to Springfield a few weeks later, I received another call from Coach Gilman who said he had changed his mind and offered me the scholarship to play football for the University of Cincinnati. I thanked Coach Gilman for the call but told him I had committed to Wittenberg and turned down his offer.

Arriving at the Wittenberg campus in early fall of 1951, I was invited to join the Alpha Tau Omega fraternity located at 40 West Cassily Street, in Springfield, a block east of the campus. When I found out the ATO's reached out to new athletes, I agreed to pledge to that fraternity. I have many good memories of living at the ATO house for two years. Tom Fluke, Danny Winters, Bill Goettman, Joe Cole and

Tom BeMiller are a few names that have stayed with me over the years.

Ironically, I never played a moment of football at Wittenberg. I had sustained a hip injury in my last year playing sports at Hazel Park High School. I was advised by a doctor in Springfield that it would be wise for me not to play any more football. I listened to the medical expert and did not play football at Wittenberg. I did however, follow the Wittenberg football team for the next four years and recorded statistics for the coaches and reported the games for the local Springfield News Sun newspaper.

Even though I couldn't play the sport that brought me to Wittenberg, I did play four years of basketball and baseball for the school. I was blessed to be able to earn seven varsity letters; four in baseball and three in basketball while attending Wittenberg University.

I enjoyed my four years of playing basketball for Wittenberg. For the most part, I played point guard which meant my chief responsibility was to get the ball to the scorers so they could put the ball in the basket. Had college statisticians kept assist statistics back in the early 50's as they do today, I no doubt would have been high on the assist list while at Wittenberg. The most points I ever scored in a single game was thirteen. I remember a game at Ohio Wesleyan where I played the entire four quarters and one over-time period and never took a shot. However, my power-forward teammate, Bill Goettman, ended with thirty-eight points (a school record) as we won 98-92.

During my sophomore year at Wittenberg, we took an east coast trip over the Christmas holidays. We played Rider, Wagner, Adelphi, and Seton Hall in a span of four to six days.

Seton Hall was ranked no. 1 in the country the night we played them on New Year's Eve in East Orange, New Jersey. The game was scheduled to be nationally televised but Seton Hall cancelled the telecast at the last moment. They realized that it would be very embarrassing if this small Ohio Lutheran College defeated the No. 1 team in the country on National TV. But if Seton Hall beat the small school, that was what was expected. Seton Hall led by three points at half time, 35-32 and came out on top 75-60. But we felt we had held our own and we were pleased with our effort. By the way, Seton Hall had two all Americans that year, Wally Dukes and Richie Regan.

As a freshman third baseman for the Wittenberg Tigers, I led the Ohio Athletic Conference in batting with a .391 average. My friend, senior Perk Robins, played first base for Wittenberg for 4 years. Perk ended the 1952 season batting .389. I would not let him forget a freshman beat him out by two percentage points.

Among the Ohio schools we played were Ohio Wesleyan, Wilmington, Capital University, Otterbein, Wooster, Baldwin-Wallace, Hiram, Oberlin, Dennison University, Marietta, and Heidelberg.

I batted .340 in my sophomore year. I batted over .300 in my final two years and we won the Ohio Conference baseball championship in 1955. I was also fortunate to be elected captain of the championship team in my senior year.

I relished playing college basketball and baseball for Coach Howard "Red" Maurer who was quite a character. But I always knew he cared about his players. At the end of my senior year at Wittenberg, I was again voted the most outstanding senior athlete. I was truly blessed. I was also honored to be elected to the Student Court and to the Blue Key Honor Society while getting an education at Wittenberg

As a result of my baseball abilities and four year college record, I received two major league baseball offers; from the St. Louis Browns and Philadelphia Phillies. However, I declined both offers because I had a wife and a young son to be responsible for.

If I had accepted one of their offers, I undoubtedly would have spent several years in the minor leagues before, if ever, being called to play in the major leagues. I just couldn't subject my young wife and infant son to that kind of life.

In the summer of 1953, I also had a try-out with the Detroit Tigers at Briggs Stadium. I did go two for five in the game played between the prospects that afternoon, but never received an offer from my home-town team.

Christmas of 1953 was the first Christmas Marvel and I spent together as a married couple. I was hired by the local post office to help deliver mail during the holidays. I was assigned to help a permanent mailman on his daily mail route. Our particular route happened to cover part of the near east side of Springfield. One home we delivered mail to was occupied by an elderly African American widow who always greeted us with a gracious smile. On Christmas Eve in that year, we didn't have enough money to buy a gift for each other. I suggested that Marvel bake a small tin of cookies and take them to my widow friend and try to make her Christmas a little brighter. As we knocked on the front door, we heard a voice inside that asked, "Who is it?" I responded, "It's your mailman," and she replied, "Come on in, honey." My friend was seated in a rocking chair which was located next to her pot-bellied stove in the middle of her dirt living room floor. When we handed her the cookies, her response of gratitude was priceless. You would have thought we had handed her the keys to a new car. Marvel and I will never forget the inner peace we received from making this dear Christian lady's 1953 Christmas a memorable event.

As we drove back to our rented apartment located in an abandoned Army barracks which cost us $22.50 per month, including most utilities, we noticed a car parked along the street which was pulling an open trailer. We found out that my parents bought us a small green couch which turned into a hide-a-bed. We knew my folks were coming to visit but had no idea that they would bring us this much needed furniture. Every time we reminisce about that 1953 Christmas, we are reminded that you cannot out- give God.

CHAPTER 5

"Meeting My Soulmate"

During the summer break of 1952 after my first year at Wittenberg, I found a job doing roofing and siding work for a local contractor back in the Detroit suburb of Hazel Park, Michigan. A friend of our family, Bill Sircy from the state of Arkansas, was living with us and also worked with me for the same contractor.

One Thursday afternoon on the way home from work, I noticed a sign on Nine Mile Road in Hazel Park that read: "YOUTH TENT REVIVAL." I said to Bill, "There may be some good looking Christian girls at this event; let's go home, shower, eat, and come back and check it out." Bill agreed.

I had just broken up with a non-Christian girl not too long before. As a believer, I knew I could not get serious with a non-Christian girl again as the Bible clearly states that we should not be unequally yoked.

As we walked into the back of the tent, we were late and the service had already started. As we seated ourselves in the rear of the tent, a young lady was on the platform singing a solo song entitled, "I Know a Name, That name is Jesus."

I don't remember what the speaker said that night as I was busy planning what I was going to say to the beautiful soloist.

As it turned out, one of the sponsors of the youth revival meetings was one of my former Sunday school teachers when I was much younger. Since he could vouch for me and my family, he introduced me to the soloist, Marvel Mae Myland. We were able to talk for a few minutes after the service before she had to leave to go back to the home where she was staying. Marvel was a student at Bethesda Bible Institute located at Van Dyke and 7 Mile Road in Detroit, Michigan. Marvel's participation in the youth revival was part of the practical part of her Bible Institute training.

The youth meetings were coming to a close on Friday evening which was my final opportunity to connect with this beautiful, blonde young lady.

At work the next day, the hours dragged by as I anxiously looked forward to seeing that soloist one more time.

On the final night of the meetings, I arrived early so as to not miss out on what could be my final opportunity to interact with Marvel. The service started, I scoured the tent, and Marvel was not present. I did not remember anything else until the service was over. My last opportunity to get to know this young lady had been lost.

As I turned to leave the tent, I saw Marvel sitting in the back row of the tent. She was there after all. Apparently, she was not feeling well on Friday evening, because of the intense heat and was not going to the final service. However, one of the youth sponsors came to the house and insisted that she attend the final night of the revival. She decided to go with him and arrived late and was seated at the rear of the tent.

In any event we met up after the service and I got up the nerve to ask to take her home. Because of the familiarity of my former Sunday school teacher, she allowed me to take her home that evening.

Over the next several days, Marvel and I would spend quite a bit of time together getting to know one another and our respective goals, aspirations, and dreams.

We found out that we had both accepted Christ as our Savior at the ages of nine and 10 respectively. We learned that we had both broken up with non-Christian friends recently. We learned that we both wanted to bring honor and glory to our Lord by whatever God chose us to do the rest of our lives. We learned that we both wanted to raise our children in a Christian home and environment where Christ was revered and honored. In short, we believed God had prepared us for one another. Accordingly, on the 13th day after we met, I asked Marvel to marry me and she accepted my proposal.

Because the most important decision of my life was made in 1942 to accept Jesus Christ and follow Him the rest of my life, I had no hesitation in asking Marvel to be my wife, the second most important decision of my life. We were married on June 27th, 1953, at Bethesda Missionary Temple in Detroit, Michigan. One of my former pastors, Reverend Everett (Peggy) Hall, drove up to the wedding from Owensboro, Ky.

and conducted the ceremony. My fiancée, Marvel, met the pastor who married us on the day of the wedding.

God has blessed our union with three wonderful children. James Kevin was born April 13, 1954 in Springfield, Ohio while I was still at Wittenberg University, Linda Michelle was born September 14, 1956 in Valparaiso, Indiana while I was in law school. Our last child, Jeffrey Kent was born April 22, 1960 in Kokomo, Indiana where I served as the City-County Planning Director. As of this writing, they have given us seven grandchildren and 19 great grandchildren.

All three of our children accepted Christ by the time they were five years of age. All three children graduated from Taylor University in Upland, Indiana. Kevin is married to Carla J. Stump. Linda is married to Norman K. Long and Jeff is married to Paula C. Ricci.

No marriage is perfect because all marriages involve imperfect people. Marvel and I celebrated our 68th wedding anniversary on June 27, 2021. We have been through many difficult situations together. However, we have never encountered a challenge that couldn't be met with God's wisdom, grace, and help. We honestly feel that we are among the most fortunate and blessed people that we know, all because of God's blessings on our lives and our families' lives.

The partial athletic scholarship I received at Wittenberg was helpful but did not cover all of my expenses such as room and board, books, miscellaneous fees and all of my tuition. Also, I married Marvel M. Myland between my sophomore and junior years at Wittenberg and God blessed us with our oldest son, James Kevin Butcher, in April of

1954. Consequently, in addition to playing two sports and carrying a 3.5 grade point average, I found it necessary to work 16 different jobs in my spare time, over the four years, to make ends meet. Among those jobs were; 1. Cleaning the field house. 2. Preparing the football and soccer fields for games. 3. Delivering mail during the Christmas holidays. 4. Refereeing middle school basketball games, and 5. Covering Wittenberg football games for the local newspaper. In addition to maintaining our apartment and helping to take care of Kevin, my wife, Marvel, was able to work part-time at Richman Brothers Clothing store in downtown Springfield.

There were nights we would go to bed not having enough bread and/or milk for the following day. We asked God to provide. On more than one occasion we would open the front door the following morning and find a quart of milk or a $5.00 bill in an envelope. To this day we do not know where those provisions came from. We know however, that God provided our every need.

Early on in my freshman year at Wittenberg, I sought out and found a small Baptist church to attend. I was able to locate Maranatha Baptist Church on the far east side of Springfield, Ohio, a city of 100,000 people. The small congregation was meeting in a basement building. At first, I had to ride two buses to get to the church on Sunday mornings. Pastor John Street and his lovely wife, Joan, opened their arms to us and we became lifelong friends until they passed away some years ago. While attending Maranatha, we were able to assist the church in building a church edifice above the ground that as far as we know, still stands today.

CHAPTER 6

"Valparaiso University Law School"

I must admit I went to college primarily to continue to play sports. But while I was there, I earned a Bachelor of Science degree.

As I entered my junior year at Wittenberg, I knew I had to declare a major. I believe I always thought that I would end up as a pastor, missionary, or some similar calling in full-time vocational ministry. But, God had a different path for me.

Dr. Melvin Laatch was my political science professor and I found his classes to be interesting and challenging. I also received good grades in his classes. Dr. Richard Schrog was my sociology professor and he likewise motivated me to do something in my life that would help people wherever and whenever the opportunity afforded itself to me. Accordingly, I had a double major, Political Science and Sociology.

In the middle of my senior year at Wittenberg, Dr. Laatch made me aware of a scholarship opportunity at Valparaiso University Law School in Valparaiso, Indiana. I applied for the scholarship since I had no other career opportunities available to me. I was awarded the scholarship and we began to make plans to move to Valparaiso, Indiana. I actually received my degree at Wittenberg on a Monday morning in June of 1955. The next afternoon at 4:00 p.m., I entered the gates at the U.S. Steel Sheet and Tin Mill in Gary, Indiana to push a broom as a custodian.

I was blessed to get a job at U. S. Steel as we needed the income to live and make it through law school. Shortly after I began working in Gary I met a fellow employee, Dan Kissinger, who invited me to visit his church, Liberty Bible Church in Chesterton, Indiana. We did visit the church and made it our home until I graduated from law school three years later. We made some life-long friends at Liberty who continue to be friends today. Pastor George Badger and the entire Liberty church family were very kind to us.

We remember in particular the Chauncy and Ruth Lenhart family who lived at 204 Fair Street in Valparaiso. Our daughter, Linda, was born at Porter Memorial Hospital in Valparaiso on September 14, 1956. The Lenhart family adopted our family (figuratively) and were there whenever we needed them for fellowship, baby-sitting, transportation, meals, etc, just to name a few. Except for Joanne (Lenhart) Wysong, (whom we still keep in touch with), the rest of the Lenhart family passed away some time ago.

Before we left Springfield, Ohio to go to Valparaiso, I was offered the position of freshman basketball coach at Valparaiso University in 1955. This was exciting since I could continue my involvement with college basketball and be paid $1500.00 per year. However, after we moved to Valparaiso I learned that I could keep my job at the steel mill during all three years of law school. This was huge since we definitely needed the money to continue my legal education and take care of our family. I had to notify the athletic director that I could not coach the Valparaiso freshman basketball team.

When law school started in the fall of 1955, I was transferred into the production planning department of U. S. Steel. They allowed me to work the midnight shift. If I finished my work prior to the end of my eight hour shift, I was allowed to study my law books until the shift ended.

Our schedule for our three years at the law school was basically as follows: 1. Go to law school during the day, 2. Come home, eat and play softball or basketball for our church in the evenings, 3. Take a nap, 4. Leave for Gary Steel Mill about 11:00 P.M., 5. Work the night shift at the mill and arrive back home early the next morning, 6. Repeat the cycle the next day.

There were several times I would fall asleep going to or from work and have minor accidents. I remember one night my car ended up in a cornfield. On another occasion, I remember getting into my car in Valparaiso and driving the 30 miles trip to the steel mill parking lot and as I turned off the key, I could not remember anything except leaving

Valparaiso. God surely had his hedge of protection around me during those days.

During our three years in Valparaiso, we rented homes at 361 ½ West Lincolnway, 704 ½ N. Morgan and 903 East Chicago Street.

I graduated from Valparaiso Law School in June of 1958. The Indiana state bar examination was coming up in approximately 45 days in Indianpolis, Indiana. We didn't have the money to pay for me to take the bar exam preparation and review course, which my other colleagues took. So, Marvel and the children went home to Toledo, Ohio to stay with her mother and step-father, Lela and George Gallant, while I holed up in the Lenhart basement for about three weeks to study for the bar exam on my own. The results were not due until mid-September of 1958.

In the meantime, I needed to find employment. Since I had never even met a lawyer in my life, I applied for a position in Huntington, Indiana as their first City-County Planning Director.

Huntington agreed to hire me for the salary of $5200 per year. They gave me my own office in the Courthouse in downtown Huntington.

In late summer of 1958, I loaded our car and a small U haul trailer with all our earthly belongings and took off for Huntington, Indiana. Somewhere around Wanatah, Indiana on U.S. Route 30, I looked into my rear view mirror in time to see our wooden toy box leave the U haul and hit in the middle of U.S. 30. It took several minutes for me to pick up the pieces and continue on to Huntington.

Shortly after I moved Marvel and the children into our apartment in Huntington, I received the much awaited letter from the Indiana State Bar Examiner which informed me that I had passed the Indiana bar examination. That was a strong indicator that God wanted me to use my legal training and law degree in ways that only He knew.

CHAPTER 7

"Huntington, Indiana"

U pon the move to Huntington, Indiana we found a small church on the north side of town in a residential district. The church, Bible Baptist of Huntington was led by Pastor Colin Jutton and his wife, Ruth. Roger and Helen Stemen were another Godly Christian couple we were blessed to meet and fellowship with in Huntington. They were one of the leading families in the Huntington church. Our friendship continued long after we left Huntington.

During my short stint as Planning Director in Huntington we were privileged to work with some good men such as Attorney Jim Bowers, Chairman of the City Plan Commission, Eldon Wetters, and County Surveyor Lynn Buzzard.

While in Huntington we were able to build our first home on Sunnydale Drive on the south side of town. The home was built by local homebuilder, Jim Brannon and it cost us $11,500. We borrowed $600 from Marvel's step-father's mother for the down payment.

Unfortunately, shortly after we were settled into Huntington County, Mayor Blackburn approached me one day asking me to do something that would violate my ethical standards. As a result, I knew I would not be able to stay in Huntington very long. Shortly after I started the planning job in Huntington, I met Ted Schulenberg, a well-respected City-County planning consultant out of Indianapolis, Indiana. Ted informed me that the city of Kokomo, Indiana had just lost their City-County Plan Director, Mr. Jim Dane. I called the Kokomo Plan Commission office and was set up with a meeting with all 18 members of the two plan commissions a few nights later.

I drove the 40 miles to Kokomo and walked into the plan commission office in the basement of the Courthouse and was introduced to the members of both commissions and the assistant Plan Director, Mr. Robert Roler. After answering questions for a couple of hours, I was offered the job on the spot as the new Plan Director of the Kokomo-Howard County Plan Commissions at a starting salary of $6000 and use of a late model station wagon. I advised the men present that my wife and I normally discuss and pray over major changes like this in our lives. Mr. Bob Harrell, Chairman of the Howard County Plan Commission pointed to an adjoining room and said, "Go to the phone, shut the door and call your wife."

Still in a state of shock, I went into the office, shut the door and called Marvel. I told her the job was mine for the taking if I wanted it. I told her I could start immediately and they really seemed very anxious for my positive response. Marvel said she would abide by my decision and I walked back to the men and told them I would accept the offer.

Some of the men who offered me that position were Morris Boyce, Chairman of the City Plan Commission, Don Snider (City Councilman), James Pickett, Howard Coblentz (City Engineer), Harold Rayl, Lotus Warden (County Surveyor), Max Smith, George Pitzer, Wayne Powell (County Commissioner), and Robert Harrell. As of this writing, I believe all of the above mentioned men are deceased. I will forever be indebted to them for the confidence they placed in me in early 1959.

CHAPTER 8

"Kokomo, Indiana"

F ollowing my acceptance of the City-County Planning position in Kokomo, I commuted to Kokomo from Huntington on a daily basis for several weeks, about 80 miles round trip.

When Huntington Pastor Jutton found out we were moving to Kokomo, he made me promise that we would attend the Bible Baptist Church located at 404 W. Jefferson Street in Kokomo before we visited any other churches. Pastor Jutton's friend and classmate from Grace Theological Seminary, Eddie Smith, from Xenia, Ohio was the pastor there. On the first Saturday after we moved to Kokomo, Marvel had a miscarriage and ended up in St. Joseph Hospital on the west side of town. However, I did attend Bible Baptist Church that first Sunday only to find out that Pastor Smith was in West Virginia for the weekend preaching at a church pastored by Stacy Davis, Jr., son of two of the founders of the Kokomo Bible Baptist Church, Stacy and Mary Davis.

The guest speaker that Sunday at Bible Baptist was a professor from Moody Bible Institute, whose name I do not recall. Much to my surprise the speaker and a couple of church members visited Marvel at the hospital that Sunday afternoon. Joe and Betty O'Banion and Ralph and Juanita Poe also visited our home a few days later. This showed our family that this was a caring church.

As the Planning Director, it was my responsibility to work with many local attorneys. One of those attorneys was a tall, stately gentleman by the name of Leroy Lacey. Lee impressed me with his integrity, his ability to represent his clients well, and just the way he handled himself. Lee and I worked together well and he was the consummate professional in every sense of the word. He was a lawyer's lawyer.

The more I observed Mr. Lacey and other attorneys such as John Pierce (both of whom are deceased), I began to think that someday I would like to practice law.

God blessed our marriage with our second son, Jeffrey Kent Butcher, on April 22, 1960, my mother's birthday. Jeff was born at St. Joseph Hospital in Kokomo with the help of trusted obstetrician and pediatrician, Dr. Frederick Schwartz (who is also deceased) who lived well into his 90's.

In 1960, an opportunity to travel on a mission trip was made available to several members of our church. I was fortunate to be able to be one of the members who traveled to the Caribbean and ministered to people on several islands. Along with associate Pastor Glenn Armstrong, his father,

Herbert Armstrong and several other members of Bible Baptist, we traveled to Haiti, Jamaica, and Puerto Rico. We were able to speak to, pray with, and encourage believers who were pursuing God in these countries. In Haiti, we observed voodoo practices in the middle of the night from a safe distance. We spoke at church services held in an orphanage and generally ministered to hundreds of people over the two-week mission trip.

During the years we spent in Kokomo, different evangelists would come to our church for revival meetings. One of our favorites was southern evangelist Jimmy Johnson. During one such crusade when Rev. Johnson was the speaker and tenor Ed Lyman was the featured soloist, God spoke to us. Marvel and I told God we would make ourselves available for full-time Christian vocation.

After many months of praying and seeking God's will for our family, we were offered a full-time position with Youth For Christ, International located in Wheaton, Illinois. I was brought on staff to be the Executive Director of a world teen convention to be held in Jerusalem in 1965. Dr. Billy Graham, a member of the board of YFCI, was to be the honorary chairman of the event.

On a Monday evening just weeks before we were scheduled to move to Illinois, Evon Hedley and Samuel Wolgemuth, two YFCI executives, came to visit Marvel and me in Kokomo. They had been sent by Dr. Ted Engstrom, President of Youth For Christ International, to tell us they needed to cancel our move to Youth For Christ since they didn't have enough funds to bring on new staff members.

Marvel and I were so exuberant about our new challenge and vocational move that Evon and Sam did not have the nerve to tell us we couldn't move to Wheaton, Illinois and come on staff with Youth For Christ International. They had to return to the home office and report their decision to Dr. Engstrom. Fortunately, they both survived their decision.

On a Sunday night in Mid-August of 1962, our church held a commissioning service for our family. Dr. Samuel Wolgelmuth, a senior staff member of YFCI, gave the challenge to our family and to the church. Dr. Wogelmuth later became president of Youth For Christ, International and remained a dear friend until he passed away several years later. His son, Daniel Wolgemuth is the president of Youth For Christ today.

We sold our home in Kokomo and moved our family to Carol Stream, Illinois and my first day on the new job was September 1, 1962.

CHAPTER 9

"Youth for Christ International"

S hortly after moving to Illinois, it was decided by the board of trustees of Youth For Christ International that the World Teen Convention to be held in Jerusalem in 1965 needed to be canceled. The leaders felt the political unrest in the mid-east was too high a risk with thousands of teenagers coming from all over the world.

As a result of the change in plans at the YFCI office, my job description was changed to general counsel and assistant stewardship representative. I had the privilege of working alongside Evon Hedley, who was the Chief Stewardship Director of Youth For Christ International. Mr. Hedley reached his 100th birthday in 2016.

During my ministry at YFCI, I had the privilege of meeting many giants of the faith including Rev. Billy Graham, one of the founders and who was on the Board of Trustees at YFCI.

That list also includes Stanley Kresge and wife of the Kresge and K-Mart store empire, Dr. Bob Cook president of King's College, Dr. Warren Wiersbe, Dr. and Mrs. Halley (author of Halley's Bible Handbook), Dr. Ted Engstrom president Of World Vision, Bob Luckey president of Houghton College and Rod Sargent of the Navigators ministries.

I was in New York City on assignment in late November 1963, and had a very important meeting with the founder of the department store chain, Mr. J.C. Penny himself. I will never forget that weekend. I met with Mr. Penny on the 34th floor of his office building in downtown New York to discuss YFCI stewardship issues. Just as I was leaving his inner office, his secretary met us at the door and whispered to me, "President Kennedy" has been shot. I will not tell Mr. Penny until I give him his medication."

As I walked out onto Times Square that night, I was met with bedlam. People were crying, screaming, running up and down the streets and most seemed to be in a state of disbelief and shock.

On the following evening, I attended a YFCI Rally on Long Island. After the meeting, I caught the subway back to my hotel across from Central Park. Before going to my room at the Central Park Hotel, I stopped for a snack at a deli across the street from the hotel. While standing in line waiting to pay for my food, an important looking man dressed in a three-piece suit asked me if I was a pastor since he saw me carrying my Bible. I replied no, but I was involved in full-time Christian ministry with Youth For Christ International. He then said he would like to know more about the Bible. I said I would be glad to discuss the scriptures with him and invited him to come with me to my hotel room across the street from Central Park.

As we entered my hotel room, I sat my food down on the table in the room. The gentleman sat his food down as well. I proceeded to take off my coat and he took off his outer coat. I then sat down with my Bible and I looked at my guest. He was in the middle of removing his shirt and pants. It became immediately clear to me that this man had ulterior motives and they didn't involve a discussion about the Bible.

I remember the next several minutes as being very intense. I began to quote scripture to him that I really didn't know I ever knew. It was surreal. My guest immediately began to put his clothes back on and told me he was a stock broker from New Canaan, Connecticut and his wife and children would be appalled if they knew what he does in New York City on weekends.

After my guest left, I quickly bolted the door shut and called Marvel back in Carol Stream, Illinois. She could hardly believe what had happened, but was grateful that her prayers for my safety had been answered again.

The position with YFCI required me to travel a great deal, sometimes weeks at a time. Marvel was at home in Illinois with our three small children and life became rather difficult at times. For example, our youngest son, Jeffrey, was severely burned by pork roast grease as the dish holding the roast exploded in Marvel's hands and covered much of his back and neck as he sat on the floor in the kitchen.

During this period of time Marvel's 54 year old mother, Lela Gallant, was in the final stages of cervical cancer in Toledo, Ohio. Marvel had been telling me for some time that she was having a difficult time coping with everything that was going on in our lives. She suggested that we go to a Christian counselor and try to get some answers for our family. I thought I didn't need any help but she may benefit from some wise Godly counsel. But I didn't take any steps to find a Christian counselor since I believed things would be better if we waited a while longer.

As I walked into our home at 443 Indianwood Drive, Carol Stream, Illinois after a lengthy absence, Marvel was taking pictures off the wall and packing them into boxes. She had decided if I wasn't going to get some help, she would take the children and go back to Toledo where her mother and step-father lived until I was ready to seek help.

Wait just a minute! She was serious about our situation. I asked her to stop packing and I would get some help for her. I immediately called the Covenant Christian Counseling Center in downtown Chicago, Illinois and arranged for an appointment to get my wife some professional help.

After we filled out a myriad of forms, we met with Dr. Truman Essau at the counseling center. Following a few introductory exchanges, Dr. Essau asked a very probing question. When he learned some of the problems going on in our lives, he asked me if I was happy in my position with YFCI. I thought for a few moments and then told him, not really because my family needed me around more and I had to travel a lot with my position. I told him I didn't know you could be totally happy and still be in God's will. That would be selfish. I believed you had to be somewhat miserable or you wouldn't be in the center of God's will for yourself or your family. But I couldn't come up with a chapter or verse for that theory.

Dr. Essau then asked me what I really wanted to do with the rest of my life. I selfishly said I wanted to practice law and get involved in politics. Dr. Essau then asked us to open our Bibles to Psalms chapter 37, and to read out loud verses three through six which read as follows: v. 3 "Trust in the LORD ..." v. 4 "Delight thyself in the LORD ..." v.5 "Commit your way to the LORD ..." v.6 "...and He will give you the desires of your "heart"

He then asked us if we had met the conditions outlined in those verses; had we trusted in the LORD, had we delighted ourselves in the LORD, had we committed our ways to the LORD?

We looked at one another and said, to the best of our abilities, we had met those conditions. Then, he asked, "Why are you not practicing law and why are you not involved in politics? In other words, God promised to give you the desires of your heart if you have trusted in Him, delighted in Him and committed your way to the LORD." It was as if someone had turned on a bright light in the room. We drove back to Wheaton to the YFCI office and I submitted my thirty days written notice of resignation to Dr. Ted Engstrom, President of YFCI. As I explained my reasoning to Dr. Engstrom and Mr. Hedley, my supervisor, they seemed to understand. As it turned out, it was not Marvel, but me, that needed the counseling.

I had no idea if, how, or where the practice of law and entry into politics would begin. We had three options. First, I could have started a law practice in Illinois since I had been admitted to practice law in Illinois in 1963. Second, we could have gone back to Springfield, Ohio where I had attended college as we liked the Springfield area and Marvel was born in Ohio and had family there. But it made the most sense to consider going back to Kokomo, Indiana where we had a lot of friends and where our dear friends Pastor Ed Smith and his wife Suzanne were still ministering at Bible Baptist Church.

When I shared our decision to leave YFCI for the reasons set out above, Pastor Smith suggested I may want to talk to L. Owen Bolinger, a local Kokomo attorney who also attended Bible Baptist Church with his wife Mary Ann on a fairly regular basis.

I did meet with Mr. Bolinger and he offered me the opportunity to work for him at a salary of $12,000 per year. I will forever be grateful to the late L. Owen Bolinger for giving me a chance to practice law.

CHAPTER 10

"Return to Indiana"

So, two years to the day we left Kokomo to move to Illinois, the Butcher family returned to Kokomo on September 1, 1964. The law office was located on the sixth floor of the Union Bank building in downtown Kokomo, one block north of the Howard County Courthouse. My personal office was probably no larger than eight feet by 10 feet, but it was adequate and I was blessed to begin the practice of law.

Because of my previous public life as the City-County Plan Director, clients began calling for appointments shortly after I hung out my sign. Many of my clients wanted me to represent them in planning and zoning matters involving issues with the Kokomo City Plan Commission, the Howard County Plan Commission, the Kokomo City Board of Zoning Appeals, and the Howard County Board of Zoning Appeals.

Mr. Bolinger was very helpful to me as I started my practice. It wasn't very long before my appointment calendar was full.

Obviously, we went back to Bible Baptist Church and resumed our fellowship with a lot of friends we had made in our earlier tenure in Kokomo. I was blessed to be given several responsibilities at the church over the next several years. I was church moderator several years, served as a deacon chairman for many years, taught several different Sunday school classes, was the first chairman of the Board of Kokomo Christian School which was started at Bible Baptist in the early 1970's, and served as chairman of the Pulpit Committee several different times. Marvel and I also served as youth sponsors at the church for many years as well. Marvel and Ruth Tharp started the Pioneer Girls ministry at the church and led many young ladies through this Christ-honoring program over many years.

During the latter part of 1967, I had a talk with Mr. Bolinger about my future with his law firm. I was making a lot of money for him well above my annual salary. I asked if I could ever become a partner with him or at least share in the profits of the firm. Even though we never had a disagreement and we worked together well, he told me he was a very private person and would never enter into a partnership with any attorney. Accordingly, I told him that I would be looking for an opportunity to open my own office. He said he understood and wished me well.

Shortly thereafter a good friend, David Greeson Jr., told me he had just noticed a building for sale on the corner of Walnut and Buckeye Streets, right across from the courthouse in downtown Kokomo. I called the realtor, Joe Pencek, as I recall, who showed me the building whose most recent tenant was the "Tots Bazaar" children's clothing store. The building was built in 1854 and is commonly known to be the oldest building in downtown Kokomo. It was 20 feet wide and 60 feet long and appeared to be the right size for my needs.

The owner, a 90 year old widow from Delphi, Indiana, wanted $20,000 for her building with $2,000 as a down payment. She wanted $150 per month with a very low interest rate. It seemed to be the perfect opportunity; just one problem, I didn't have any money!

David Greeson offered to loan me $5,000 to help buy the building and prepare the office for receiving clients. After I paid the down payment, that left $3,000 to remodel the building, buy office equipment and furniture, purchase legal stationary and hang a sign on the front of the building: James R. Butcher, Attorney at law.

Floyd Williams, a good friend from church, did the remodeling including lowering the ceiling and enclosing my office space as well as the secretary's office. Remodeling also included new plumbing, heating, electrical system, air conditioning and carpet. In addition to the remodeling, we stretched that last $3,000 to provide everything we needed to open the doors to the public on January 2, 1968.

Another dear friend from church, Eugene McCarty, his wife Vivian, and Marvel and I and our children moved all of the furniture, equipment and miscellaneous items needed to open a law office in sub-zero temperature on New Years' day 1968. I still can't believe we were able to stretch the money we had available to accomplish what was needed to open a new law office.

We have lived in "the City of Firsts" continually since 1964. We have made many wonderful friends. Over the years, God gave me several opportunities to help initiate several organizations for the betterment of our community.

With the help, encouragement, and assistance of several Godly men such as Seymour Zwirn, Dr. Bob Blue, Steve Johnson, Dr. Bob Clements, Charles Kibler, Eric Harvey, Leroy and Lewis Colter and several other men whose names escape me as of this writing, we founded the Kokomo Chapter of the Kokomo Christian Business Men's Association. We met weekly for several years to hear various Christian speakers and fellowship and encourage men in their Christian walks. One of the favorite speakers was Charles "Tremendous" Jones who was a challenging speaker from Harrisburg, Pennsylvania.

We also founded a local Youth For Christ chapter in Kokomo in 1965. This group of believers held Saturday night rallies for teenagers of Howard County and the surrounding area. The meetings were held in the local high school auditorium and the Courtland Avenue Friends Church. Many teenagers came to faith in Christ during the years YFC ministered in this area.

Noticing a real need in downtown Kokomo several years ago, several local businessmen started "Frontline For Jesus" to help people struggling with drug and other addictions. We bought a building on North Buckeye, just north of my law office. For several years we ministered to many young adults as they came to us for help dealing with their various addictions.

In 1970, I recognized the lack of a summer baseball program in our area for boys in the 16 – 18 year age category. I talked to several other men in the area to start a program for these young men that were not quite good enough to play for the local American Legion team who only carried 18 players on the roster.

Several local businessmen including, but not limited to, Jerry Fiscus, Joe Shoffner, Bob Ricci, Cy Meyers, Clair Stark and Don Everman along with Judges Carl Van Dorn and Bob Kinsey, started the Senior Boys baseball league, playing games at Kautz field in downtown Kokomo, Highland Park stadium and Carver Center. We didn't have much money, so we sold cold drinks out of the trunk of a car before and during games. The board members and managers and coaches prepared the fields for play by cutting the grass and placing lime on the foul lines with a tin can.

The early teams were sponsored by East Side Barber Shop, Shoffner Kitchens, City-Cab, RayWel Motors and Western Southern Insurance. Eventually, we joined the National Connie Mack baseball organization.

Dozens of young men played in this program for about 25 years. It seems like I run into a former Connie Mack player every few months. They all seem to have great memories of their involvement in this summer baseball program.

I was blessed to have served on the board of the Kokomo Rescue Mission for 13 years (now an emeritus member), served on the board of CEF (Child Evangelism Fellowship), was Co-Founder, and first president and served on the board for twenty-five years of The Indiana Family Institute, an affiliate of Focus on the Family. Along with my dear friend Eric Miller, I was privileged to help found Citizens Concerned for The Constitution (now Advance America), a pro-America and pro-Christian organization operating out of Indianapolis, Indiana.

CHAPTER 11

"Practice of Law"

From day one, September 1, 1964, until I retired, I never lacked for business. God has abundantly brought people into the office over the years and I will be eternally grateful.

My first secretary was Jane Everman, and she stayed with the office for several years.

In 1973, God sent another lawyer, David R. Ball to join my practice. David was a very good advocate for his clients for 26 years until he passed away a few years ago. David was also a pastor of an apostolic church in Carmel, Indiana. He would practice law four days a week and handle his pastoral duties three days a week. As far as I can remember David and I never had a disagreement. It was a blessing to work with this fine lawyer and better person. We also shared our love of basketball by playing three noon hours per week at the YMCA two blocks east of the office.

In 1976, a gentleman named R. Alan Brubaker walked into my office. He had learned about me from a mutual friend, song evangelist, Ed Lyman, from the state of Tennessee. Alan and Ed had met in church in the Panama Canal Zone where Alan was stationed with the U.S. Army's Judge Advocate General Program. Shortly after our first visit, Alan decided to leave the service and begin the practice of law. Alan became a part of Butcher, Ball, and Brubaker in the fall of 1976. Alan later left the practice to become a judge in the Howard County Indiana Circuit Court. Alan and his wife, Peggy, and family remain good friends of our family.

In 1979, I met Jeffrey A. Lowry, a nephew of Alan R. Brubaker, who was enrolled in Dayton, Ohio University Law School at the time. Jeff began interning in our office that summer and became a valued law partner until my retirement. Over the years, several other attorneys have worked in our office for varying periods of time. Steve Kincaid, Bill P. Heck, Mark Hurt, and Justin Alter have all contributed to the success of our law practice. At the time of this writing, Joshua McMahan is the third attorney in our office and Scott McClelland joined us in January 2016.

Some other interesting facts about the law office include the murder that took place in what is now the lobby. In 1866, Mayor Milton Cole shot and killed his wife's lover and he himself was murdered a few years later in Anderson, Indiana.

In the late 1990's, I was privileged to work as a Deputy Prosecutor in Cass County under the supervision of my good friend, Prosecutor Rick Maughmer. I enjoyed that opportunity for approximately ten years.

Over the years, we expanded our original space by acquiring the small beauty shop located to the west of our building, and by buying the two properties located to the north of our original building. One was an office that housed the offices of Kokomo Police Department detective division, including the polygraph room. We also bought out what had been the Kokomo City Cab office for many years. Each time we would acquire another property, we would knock holes in the walls to allow for our expansions. We were also able to acquire another property which adjoins the alley to the north of our office and is used for office personnel parking.

I would be remiss if I didn't mention some of the ladies God sent to our office to serve as legal assistants. Judith A. Buck served as office manager for 41 years and made major contributions to the overall success of the law firm. Teresa Harvey and Beth Smith have been with the office for well over 38 years each. They are the primary legal assistants in the field of personal injuries and estates. Much of the firm's success over the years is directly attributed to the loyalty and multiple skills of these two ladies. Donna Crowell served as Mr. Ball's legal assistant until his death and then worked for Mr. Lowry for many years. Donna retired in 2014. For 23 years, Terri Gingerich served me well with her skills as my practice evolved into serving the needs of the elderly in central Indiana. Gail Ambrose is another lady who served our office faithfully for about 15 years. The following ladies also contributed to the success of our law firm over the years; Linda Koontz, Tammy (Helm) Ralstin, Darlene Newburn Bochman, Donna Brock, Deb McDaniels, Kathryn

Rubalcaba, Destry Richey, Lori Slabaugh, Terri Layton, Karen Cole, Beth Ann Gibson, Micki Jones, Carla Barker, Sheila Haulter, Kathy Davis, Andrea Murray, Lindsay Brown, Bridgette Welsh, and Jennifer Jack. Several of our grandchildren interned in our office over the years as well. I may have omitted some of the women who have worked in our office and made contributions to our success. I do apologize.

CHAPTER 12

"Entering Politics"

U pon our return to Kokomo in the fall of 1964, I started to enter the political arena primarily by supporting other good, conservative candidates for public office. I knew that the time would arrive when I should throw my "hat into the ring" and actually run for an office.

That opportunity arrived in 1977. Our Congressman, Elwood ("Bud") H. Hillis, had been serving our district for around 16-18 years. In the spring of 1978, Congressman Hillis, several other conservative local republicans, and I, determined it was time for a change in our own local county Republican leadership. It was believed by many of us that our current chairman of the local party, attorney Ralph Helms, needed to be replaced for the good of the party. That could only be done at the local precinct level by voting him out of office and bringing in fresh leadership. I ran for precinct committeeman along with several others who felt a change was needed, but I lost my race to a Helms supporter, David Hendrickson. We were not able to garner enough votes to remove Mr. Helms from office at that time.

Our State Senator in 1978 was Democrat Merton Stanley who had been our Circuit Court Judge at one time and was also a former chairman of the Indiana Senate Finance Committee, arguably the most powerful position in the Senate other than the President Pro Tem. His committee controlled the purse strings of the state. Mr. Stanley had also been chairman of the Indiana Public Service Commission. In mid-July of 1978, former Republican Mayor John W. Miller, who was running against Senator Stanley, suddenly decided to drop out of the race. A friend of mine, Steven Johnson, who loved politics, stopped me one day in the parking lot of the local license branch and asked me if I would be willing to run against Senator Stanley in the fall of 1978. Knowing I was not a favorite of county chairman Helms, I told Steve I would never get the chairman's needed approval and therefore should probably decline. Besides that, there were only a few days to get me approved by the county chairman as the deadline to get on the ballot was the last day of August. Steve, who ironically succeeded me as a state Senator years later, asked for my permission to contact the chairman and much to my great surprise, Mr. Helms approved placing me on the fall ballot to face two term state Senator Stanley. I later learned from the State of Indiana Republican Party Chairman, Bruce Melchert, that Helms believed I would be defeated so badly that I would be out of his hair forever. Knowing I had little to lose and a lot to gain and believing it was God's will for me to run, I accepted the challenge.

Although I was now on the state ballot for the November election, we had just two months to do the following:

1. Find a competent committee chairman;
2. Select and motivate campaign committee members;
3. Raise a minimum of $20,000.00;
4. Locate and energize an army of volunteers;
5. Set up and staff a campaign office; and
6. Get name recognition throughout the district in several counties.

Senator Stanley had the following going for him:
1. Name recognition;
2. Notoriety;
3. Experience;
4. Money;
5. An organization; and
6. Friends in high places.

Although the odds were overwhelmingly in favor of the incumbent Senator, an astonishing thing happened on November 4, 1978; We Won!! How did it happen?

The selection of a committee chairman, was in my opinion, the key to success. We asked a close Christian friend, Seymour "Cye" Zwirn, to accept that responsibility. "Cye", in his quiet but efficient manner, gave us the leadership that was desperately needed. With "Cye's" guidance, we were able to mobilize hundreds of volunteers who knocked on doors, manned phone banks, mailed out campaign materials, and generally motivated dozens of people to vote who had not been accustomed to voting in local elections.

No doubt my leadership position in my own church, my lay speaking in churches and other Christian organizations, and being one of the founders of the local Youth For Christ organization, Christian Business Men's Committee, and Front Line for Jesus ministry, and serving as an active board member of the local Child Evangelism organization and Rescue Mission assured voters that I would represent them and their values and not deviate from my Christian convictions on issues with moral implications.

Senator Stanley had been the author of Indiana's No Fault Divorce bill in 1973. Indiana was the second state in the country, after California, to pass this legislation. I was determined to do my best to help repeal the "No-Fault Divorce" law in Indiana. The law just made it too easy to break up a marriage, a home, and a family regardless of the negative consequences to family members, especially children. Unfortunately, I was not able to repeal Indiana's No-Fault Divorce law in my eight year tenure in the Senate. But I was successful in authoring and helping pass a new Legal Separation bill which gives Hoosier couples another alternative to divorce.

During my eight year stint as a State Senator I was very fortunate to serve on several important committees. I served on the Senate Economic Development Committee, the powerful Senate Finance Committee and I served as chair of the Senate Ethics Committee.

I was blessed with the ability to author or co-author about 110 bills that became law in my two terms in the Senate. Some of the more important bills that I authored were the following, to-wit:

1. "Guilty, but mentally ill", to allow people found guilty of a major crime, but mentally ill, to serve their time in a mental medical facility, but not be let out on the street again as a result of the plea or findings.
2. "The Baby Doe" bill to protect viable, but imperfect, new born infants.
3. A Law which requires girls under 18 years of age to get parental or guardian permission for an abortion.
4. A bill requiring children to be at least 12 years of age before they can purchase cigarettes.
5. A bill which increases a child's exemption from $2,000 to $5,000 before they will be required to pay any inheritance taxes on assets left to them by their parents.

In 1982, I ran for re-election against Joe Harris, local labor leader and former State Representative. This time we had to raise $40,000 to fund the campaign. Seymour Zwirn once again served as chairman and did a fabulous job to bring us to victory in another hard fought and close race.

One of my top campaign volunteers, Jan Buechler, happened to attend the same church as Mr. Harris. Shortly, after our November 1982 victory, Jan began receiving pornographic videos, magazines and erotic material in her home mailbox. We loaded my car trunk with these unwanted materials and delivered them to the postmaster in Indianapolis, Indiana. I was able to procure Mr. Harris' signature from financial documents filed previously in the statehouse. It didn't take the postmaster in Indianapolis very long to determine that these materials were ordered by former State Representative Joe Harris, who was irate that Mrs. Buechler had played a key role in our 1982 repeat victory for the Indiana State Senate.

During my eight year tenure in the state senate, I was able to secure funding for the $2 million dollar cost of widening Markland Avenue, in Kokomo, Indiana, the main east-west artery in town, which was desperately needed.

One of the highlights of my Senate career was going to the 1980 Republican National Convention in my home town, Detroit, Michigan. I went as an alternate delegate with Marvel and spent considerable time on the convention floor. This was the time and place Ronald Reagan received the Republican nomination for President of the United States. I had never felt so proud to be an American.

I had the privilege of serving in the state Senate under two great Governors, Dr. Otis Bowen and Robert Orr. Governor Orr was kind enough to grant me a Sagamore of the Wabash Award in 1986, one of the highest honors that can be awarded to an Indiana resident for outstanding service to the state.

Also, in the years after I left the Indiana Senate, Governor Orr appointed me to become the chairman of The State Ethics Commission where we handled ethical issues for about 35,000 state employees.

After U.S. Senator Dan Quayle was chosen by Presidential candidate George H. W. Bush to be his Vice Presidential running mate, I was one of ten men interviewed by Gov. Orr to replace Dan Quayle as a U. S. Senator. I was honored to be considered as a replacement for Senator Quayle.

Another highlight of my state senate tenure was a chance to become affiliated with the American Legislative Exchange Council. The council is a national organization with an office in Washington, D. C. which assists conservative legislators in all 50 states with conference training sessions to help prepare for the battles with liberal organizations and legislators.

Another benefit of belonging to ALEC was the frequent opportunity to meet and spend time with national conservative leaders such as Congressmen Jack Kemp (R), New York, Phil Crane (R), Illinois, former President Gerald Ford and Congressman Newt Gingrich. The highlight of my affiliation with ALEC was to spend, along with seven other state legislators from around the country, 45 minutes with President Ronald Reagan in a private meeting room in the Tampa, Florida airport. I sat three feet away from the most powerful and important man in the world. I was impressed with his humility, wit and friendliness. I shall never forget that day in 1986.

In 1983, the world Zionist organization invited eight ALEC members to visit Israel at their expense. Again, I was one of eight state legislators across the country offered this opportunity. Among the highlights of that trip was the opportunity to spend some quality time with Menachem Begin, Prime Minister of the nation of Israel. I gave him an

Indiana lapel pin and assured him there were a lot of Indiana residents praying for him and his country. He retired shortly after our visit.

We were also given the opportunity to have a sit-down meeting with the Palestine Liberation Organization (PLO). We sat in a small room with these men with their guns draped over their laps. We were able to ask questions and interact with these enemies of Israel for approximately 30 minutes.

CHAPTER 13

"Run for Congress"

In early 1985, eight term Congressman Elwood H. "Bud" Hillis of Howard County made it known that he was not going to run for re-election. Almost immediately sitting Indiana State Treasurer, Julian Ridlen, Republican, from Logansport, Indiana, let it be known that he aspired to fill the vacancy. In addition, there were three other men who decided to throw their names into the hat in the 1986 spring primary election. One of those men was Jim Pearson, a Mayor from Crown Point who had plenty of name recognition in the northern part of the district. The fifth district at the time ran from eastern Grant County north and west to include the southern part of Lake County, Indiana.

After considerable prayer, discussions with family members and trusted friends and advisors, I believed it was

God's will for me to make myself available to represent the 5th Congressional district of Indiana in Washington, D.C.

We formed a campaign committee chaired by a Marion Christian businessman by the name of Malcolm Evans. Craig Dunn, a long-time friend, former high school football teammate of our son, J. Kevin Butcher, and well-respected financial advisor from Kokomo, accepted the responsibility as chair of the finance committee.

The next 16 to 18 months were spent non-stop to raise name recognition, raising $500,000 to run the campaign, and participating in candidate forums and debates and public appearances at county fairs, parades, and party functions, in 16 different counties. We also had to locate, motivate, and set up local committees in each county across the district.

We were blessed with many people in each county who stepped up to the plate and worked tirelessly for our campaign. Our good friend from Lake County, Indiana, Al Evans and my fellow state Senator, Bill Costas and his extended family from Valparaiso, Indiana, were very helpful in the northern part of the state.

Congressman Hillis had never raised more than $125,000 in any of his campaigns. But we found that it took $500,000 to carry out our campaign, a full-time staff, and obviously included television and radio ads.

The primary race was difficult but we were fortunate to come out victorious over the other four qualified candidates.

We found it necessary to campaign full-time seven days a week for the entire campaign. There was a six-month period where I was not able to attend our home church one time. I was blessed to speak at many other churches throughout the district during the campaign.

We were also blessed to have a lot of prominent people get involved in our campaign. Included in that list were Congressman Phil Crane (R) Illinois, Congressman Guy Vandergagt (R) Michigan, President Gerald Ford who spoke at a breakfast for me and raised $18,000, U.S. Senator Richard Lugar who appeared with me at various functions, U.S. Senator Dan Quayle, Vice President George H. W. Bush, who campaigned for me in northern Indiana, and numerous State of Indiana public officials, too numerous to list. V. P. Bush campaigned for me in Gary, Indiana at the U.S. Steel Sheet and Tin Mill where I worked while in law school and I was privileged to then fly back to Indianapolis to another event on Air Force Two, the plane where Vice President Lyndon Johnson was sworn in as President in 1963.

My friend, the late Charles (Chuck) Colson, founder of Prison Fellowship Ministries, was very supportive of my campaign although he had to be very careful because of his position with the ministry.

Well known Gospel singing duo, Bill and Gloria Gaither, endorsed Julian Ridlen because of their Anderson University connection, before the primary was held. I contacted Bill Gaither and he agreed to have a breakfast meeting in Alexandria, Indiana, to hear my testimony and he said he would back off his endorsement of Julian Ridlen.

The democrat challenger I had to face in the fall was former state Senator, James "Jim" Jontz. I knew Jontz from my days in the legislature and knew him to be a tireless campaigner. In fact, Jim would ride a bicycle in parades which caused him to stand out. Jim Jontz was also a social and fiscal liberal which gave the voters a clear choice since I am a social and fiscal conservative.

I believe I needed State Treasurer Julian Ridlen's help if I was going to be successful in the fall of 1986. I made an appointment with Ridlen at his state house office in early August to ask for his support. He told me he would not support anyone who would bring in televangelist Pat Robertson to help in a political campaign. It is true that Pat Robertson called our campaign office and asked if he could come in and raise money for me with no strings attached. I certainly appreciated the offer and he flew in for a whole day of meetings and raised $35,000 for our campaign. I will be eternally grateful for Pat's time and effort. While I don't necessarily agree with all of his theology, I do admire him as a man of God who is genuine in his beliefs and conduct. During the approximate eight to ten hours Pat was in Indiana that day speaking at various events and receptions, he never once even mentioned his ministries, programs, etc., but concentrated on finding out about me, my family, my aspirations, the campaign, etc. He showed me what a gracious, humble man he was. He was the second person to call and congratulate me on my primary victory and the second person to call to console me after my defeat in the fall of 1986.

As we neared the fall election, all the polls had us winning. However, Jim Jontz came out with a TV ad near the end of the campaign that may have hurt me. He showed a scene from the Indiana Senate floor where I was absent for a few votes. He was insinuating that I had not been attentive to senate matters and really was not doing a good job for my constituents. The truth is that before the day I missed a few votes, I had cleared my absence with the President Pro Tem Robert Garton of the Senate and the few bills that were voted on that afternoon were mundane matters that passed 48-1 or 47-2. I had voted on the important bills that morning before I flew out to a fundraiser in Washington, D.C. Ironically, my voting record in the eight years I was in the senate was about 98% and my attendance record was around 97% to 98%. The ad was clever and apparently effective in spite of being misleading.

On election evening we gathered at our campaign office in downtown Kokomo. TV channels 6, 8, and 13 were present. A few moments before it became evident that Jim Jontz was our next congressman for our 5th district, our pastor son, Kevin, took me aside and asked this question, "Dad, what are you going to say if you come in second tonight?" I replied, "Kevin, I haven't given any thought about that since all the polls have us winning."

Once we had the results from several of the larger counties, we knew I had lost the election. I was asked to address the media but before I spoke, I asked Kevin to come to the podium and pray for our new congressman. Kevin did as asked.

Sometime later that evening Kevin gave me some sage counsel. He said, "Dad, if you ran this congressional race with integrity, worked as hard as you could to win and didn't compromise your values and still didn't win the race, you are not a LOSER, you just came in second." He went on to say, "Dad, most of the great apostles and heroes of the New

Testament were beheaded or crucified for the cause of Christ. The world would call them losers, but in God's economy, they were winners." The more I thought about the outcome, the more Kevin's remarks made sense. On the next Sunday at his church, Grace Baptist Church in Montpelier, Indiana, Kevin preached a sermon titled, "Learning from Defeat." I have shared that message with others who have lost a political race. Frankly, I felt worse for the many people across the district, including numerous older folks, who gave so tirelessly of their time, finances and energy for the campaign. Many were deeply disappointed and let me know so. I shall always be grateful and indebted to them.

The loss was hard to explain. We had raised enough money, we had a great committee, a good campaign plan, enough volunteers, the right message, two good assistants that lived with us through the primary and the fall campaign; Bill Bock, a sharp young Christian pre-law candidate and then Mike Green who handled the last half of the campaign. Our over-all campaign manager was Mike Young from Indianapolis. Mike was great to work with. He has stayed in politics and has been an Indiana state Senator for several years. Several months after the loss, Brad Tate, a friend at our church, Bible Baptist Church of Kokomo, Indiana, told me why I lost. He said, "Jim, I know how badly you wanted to go to Washington, D.C. and thought it was part of God's plan for your life. However, I know you well enough to know above all other desires, you wanted God's will to be done in this matter." My friend Brad was right, <u>God's will and plan</u> was uppermost in my heart.

CHAPTER 14

"Life after Congressional Race"

Since the 1986 Congressional loss we have come to believe it was not God's will for me to go to Washington D.C. for several years and not be around for our seven grandchildren whom God has blessed us with. As much as I wanted to win and as much as I wanted to be a Congressman, the Lord knew I wanted His will to be accomplished above everything else.

Marvel and I now have been blessed with seven grandchildren and 19 great grandchildren.

In 1985 and 1986, several of our grandchildren were just being born. As I look back over the years since the election loss, Marvel and I have been privileged to be an integral part of their lives. Vacations to the Grand Cayman Islands, Pompano Beach, Marco Island, and other similar trips with the entire family have been wonderful bonding and teaching opportunities.

Whenever possible we made it a priority to be present at dance recitals, cheerleading, choir and drama performances, tennis matches, track and field events, soccer games, and baseball, football and basketball games. These events took us all over central Indiana from Kokomo to Columbus, Bloomington, Martinsville, New Palestine, Carmel, Beech Grove, Speedway, and many other communities. We've also traveled across southern Michigan and as far as Philadelphia, Pennsylvania and Denver, Colorado to be present for special events in our grandchildren's lives.

All seven of our grandchildren came to a saving faith in Jesus Christ at early ages. All seven have graduated from Christian Universities. Six of our grandchildren are married and five married Christian mates they met at Taylor University in Upland, Indiana.

It has become increasingly apparent to Marvel and me, that being available to build into the lives and character of our seven grandchildren and our great grandchildren would not have been possible had I won the congressional race and we moved to Washington, D.C. God knew from the beginning that being available for our grandchildren in their formative years was infinitely more important than winning an election. As I have gradually grasped this truth over the years, it helped me understand what is truly more satisfying than winning a hard-fought election.

In 1988, Kokomo, Indiana, was littered with five adult bookstores. A local pastor, Pat Schwanbachler, of St. Luke's United Methodist Church, called my law office and asked for an appointment. He stated he had just moved to Kokomo from the Duluth, Minnesota area where they were successful in closing down the adult bookstores and similar outlets. He mentioned the blight he observed in Kokomo, namely the five adult bookstores, three on the U. S. 31 by-pass and two downtown. I told him we had tried a few years earlier but were unsuccessful in shutting down these businesses.

I agreed to set up a meeting in my law office with some other pastors and concerned citizens. We began to meet every other Thursday at 4:30 p.m. in the conference room in our law office in downtown Kokomo to pray and plan. We organized planned walks, marches, and prayer vigils around the courthouse and some of the bookstores.

We formed a legal entity called Citizens For Decency and asked Chief of Police Bob Sargent, Sheriff J.D. Beatty and Howard County Prosecutor James Andrews to get involved and take whatever steps were necessary to rid the community of this blight.

I invited Prosecutor Andrews to visit the adult bookstore on the north side of Kokomo to observe first-hand what kind of illegal activity was taking place. I offered to drive and I backed my green Buick up to the building so no one would see my license plate.

We walked in as if we were customers and surveyed the explicit written and video materials that were available to purchase. Then, we visited the back-rooms where the sexual activity takes place. The stench was overwhelming and we quickly exited the building. I asked Mr. Andrews if he wanted to visit another adult facility and he said, "I've seen enough!"

The Prosecutor, Sheriff and Chief of Police then collaborated to send several wired under-cover detectives into several of the bookstores to observe first-hand the solicitation for sex and the illegal activities that were taking place. Several arrests of customers and store personnel were carried out which culminated in all five illegal adult bookstores being closed.

Eighteen months after we started, all five bookstore owners appeared in a packed Howard County Circuit Court room to plead "no contest." Judge R. Alan Brubaker, my former law partner, ordered all signs removed from all five facilities within 30 days. It was another example of what a few dedicated and motivated people can accomplish with a prayerful sense of urgency and dedication. Had I been in Washington D.C. the bookstores may still be flourishing in our community.

Possibly another reason why I ran for congress didn't show up until about 2011. One day in 2011, I received a phone call from Nadia Schloss. In 1986, Nadia was the State Chairperson of Indiana Right to Life, residing in Lake County, Indiana, and was very supportive and helped in our congressional efforts in Lake and Porter counties.

I had not heard from Nadia since 1986, and I was surprised at her call. She told me that she and some of her children would be coming to Kokomo in a few days and asked if she might stop by the office for a few minutes. "Of course," I told Nadia, who arrived a few days later and I invited them into my private office. As we sat around the table and rehashed the 1986 congressional campaign, Nadia floored me with her next statement. She said she watched me in all kinds of venues and circumstances during the congressional campaign. She said she observed what I did and said throughout the course of the campaign and saw a genuine Christian "who walked the talk." Accordingly, although she had been involved in her church for years, she had now received Jesus as her personal Lord and Savior in part, because of the way I lived out my faith. Nadia, her husband and children, were now walking with the Lord and worshipping at a Bible centered church. Could this possibly be another reason why I ran for the U.S. Congress?

CHAPTER 15

"Glory Road"

Several years ago, a film came out that was entitled "Glory Road." It was a story of how in 1966, a college basketball team from Texas Western University consisting of black players played and beat the University of Kentucky basketball team whose players were all white. The event was memorable for many reasons, but one was that the all-black team beat the Kentucky team in the 1966 National College Championship game in Lexington, Kentucky. But more importantly, the event opened the door on a national scale for black athletes to be allowed to compete and do so quite impressively.

Marvel and I went to the Kokomo theater complex as this was a movie I really wanted to see. After the film concluded, my mind went back to my basketball days at Wittenberg University in Springfield, Ohio, from 1951 to 1955. Our varsity basketball squad of twelve athletes consisted of eleven white players and one black athlete named Charles "Chuck" Henry.

Chuck was a pre-theological major at Wittenberg and felt called of God to preach the gospel and serve as a pastor to a local congregation.

Chuck was not only a very good basketball player, but he was a person who always had a smile on his face. I don't ever remember "Chuck" having a negative word about his white teammates or anybody else.

I hadn't heard from or about Charles "Chuck" Henry since we both left Wittenberg. On the way home after viewing "Glory Road", I confided to my wife that I had some unfinished business to address. When she asked for further details, I told her," I have sinned against my teammate and brother, Charles "Chuck" Henry, back in the early 1950's."

I shared that when our basketball team played games south of the Ohio River my teammate and brother in Christ, Chuck Henry, was treated as slaves had been treated in the south years ago. As we traveled to Kentucky to play Berea College and Transylvania, Chuck had to enter the back door of the restaurants we visited and eat in the kitchen as the rest of the team was served in the regular dining room of the restaurant. Also, Chuck could not stay at the hotel where the team stayed, but at a facility for African-American folks.

The Wittenberg basketball team, me included, and the coaching staff, trainers, and manager did nothing to "stop" or "mitigate" the treatment our teammate was receiving. We just accepted it as the way it was going to be in America in the early 1950's.

This kind of behavior wouldn't be tolerated today in any state in the country, because it is not only illegal but immoral. But, it did happen while our entire basketball team and coaching staff watched and did nothing.

God prompted my heart during the movie that I had a problem of long standing to take care of.

Upon returning home, I began a search for my former teammate and found Chuck pastoring a church in Evansville, Indiana. When I reached Pastor Henry on the phone I said, "Chuck, my friend and brother, I owe you a very late apology for allowing you to be treated like a second-class person and citizen, and for that I will be eternally sorry and beg your forgiveness." Without hesitation, Chuck acknowledged my deep remorse and forgave me for my thoughtless and Godless behavior so many years ago.

About 18 years ago, several business men in Kokomo started a men's Bible study, entitled, "The Huddle." Anywhere from 100 to 175 men meet every Wednesday at noon for lunch during the school year at the local YMCA to hear a speaker and then discuss the talk with other men on how to apply the Biblical truths learned in our everyday lives.

Shortly after Chuck and I had our "come to Jesus" telephone conversation, I invited Chuck and his lovely wife to come to Kokomo and share his heart and visit the men of Huddle.

Chuck and Mrs. Henry came to Kokomo a few weeks later and he spoke to a large group of men about his life and walk with the Lord. I will never forget the line of 12-15 men who stayed after the talk was over to be prayed for by this incredible man of God.

I may never see Charles "Chuck" Henry again in this life, but I know I will spend eternity with this dear brother. I sleep a lot better at night knowing that my friend and former college teammate showed me grace and mercy when I finally made things right with him after more than fifty years.

CHAPTER 16

"President Abraham Lincoln"

There came a time during our early years in Kokomo, that I met a tall, stately, white-headed gentleman by the name of Oliver Ransopher. Mr. Ransopher was a pastor of the small Forest, Indiana, Baptist Church for many years and also served as curator at the Howard County, Indiana Museum in downtown Kokomo. Rev. Ransopher also was an Abraham Lincoln collector and spoke about our 16th President throughout schools in the mid-western states for several years.

Upon Rev. Ransopher's passing, in his late 80's, I felt that I should make myself available to keep the life and memories of President Lincoln alive in the center of the state of Indiana. Accordingly, I began speaking at schools, churches, service clubs and to anybody who would listen, as President Lincoln, in full costume, including his black three-piece suit, full beard, and tall black hat.

As I prepared to speak on President Lincoln, I began to acquire and read all the books, pamphlets, articles, letters, etc., on Lincoln's life that I could find. I also visited several museums and libraries such as the Lincoln library in Fort Wayne, Indiana and the Lincoln Memorial University and library at Harrogate, Tennessee.

There came a time when I was drawn into a deeper quest to research President Lincoln's spiritual walk and his relationship with God, if in fact, it existed. After reading many books and other written materials, I concluded (without any reservations) that President Lincoln invited Jesus Christ to be his Savior, as he stood on the battlefield at Gettysburg in November of 1863.

A book written by Frank Crosby, a Philadelphia attorney, entitled "Life of Abraham Lincoln", was published within three months after Lincoln's assassination in 1865. The writer wrote on page 390, "Honored as a private citizen, happy in his domestic relations, successful as a statesman, he was, moreover, an avowed Christian. He often said that his reliance in the gloomiest hours was on his God, to whom he appealed in prayer, although he had never become a professor of religion. To a clergyman who asked him if he loved his Savior, he replied: "When I was first inaugurated, I did not love him; when God took my son I was greatly impressed, but still I did not love him; but when I stood upon the battle-field of Gettysburg I gave my heart to Christ, and I can say now I do love the Savior."

Many subsequent authors and Lincoln biographers have confirmed the time and place where President Lincoln entered into an eternal relationship with his God, through His Son, Jesus Christ.

In 1920, John Wesley Hill, D. D., LL.D., chancellor of Lincoln Memorial University in Harrogate, Tennessee, wrote "Abraham Lincoln, Man of God." In Chapter XXVIII, on pages 294 and 295, Dr. Phineus Gurly, President Lincoln's pastor during his last years as President, stated, "...I have had frequent and intimate conversations with him (President Lincoln) on the subject of the Bible and of the Christian religion, when he could have no motive to deceive me, and I consider him sound, not only in the truth of the Christian religion, but on all the fundamental doctrines and teachings; and more than that, in the later days of his chastened and weary life, after the death of his son, Willie, and his visit to the battlefield of Gettysburg, he said, with tears in his eyes, that he had lost confidence in everything but God, and that he now believed his heart was changed and that he loved the Savior."

During my research into President Lincoln's spiritual pilgrimage, I found numerous other well documented accounts confirming his life–changing encounter with Jesus Christ on the battlefield of Gettysburg.

As I continued my research into the life and times of President Lincoln, I came up with some very interesting comparisons with my own life.

For example, both Lincoln's parents and my parents were born in slave states, Kentucky and Tennessee, and subsequently moved north to Union states, Indiana and Michigan. Both President Lincoln and I moved from Indiana to the state of Illinois. Both President Lincoln and I were lawyers and we both served in our respective state legislatures. President Lincoln's wife was named Mary and my wife's name is Marvel. Both sets of parents were Christians and affiliated with the Separate Baptist denomination as a result of their up-bringing as children in southern states. Both President Lincoln's mother and my mother were major influences upon their sons in our respect for the Bible as paramount for faith and practice. We both observed the faithful prayers of our mothers for their sons that we would follow God in our lives.

Unfortunately, there is where the comparisons cease. We both ran the U.S. Congress; Lincoln won and I came in second.

There were four major books that shaped Abraham Lincoln's life. First the Bible was read and memorized by the 16th president for much of his life. It gave him direction for major decisions in his life. Second, he had great love and respect for Parson Weems', "Life of George Washington" which taught him his love of his country and patriotism.

Third, Aesop's Fables, which taught him his love for humor and funny stories. Finally, the book, Pilgrim's Progress, taught our 16th President his ability to live a life with respect for Biblical principles and values.

Among the dozens of books in my Lincoln library, the above four books were used regularly in giving Lincoln presentations, especially to school groups. Three of my books, the Bible (1812), The Life of George Washington, and Aesop's Fables, are old enough to have been personally used by Lincoln. "Pilgrim's Progress," written by John Bunyan, was bought and used during my college days at Wittenberg University in Springfield, Ohio, in the early 1950's.

I have not given Lincoln presentations in full dress and costume for a few years. However, I have continued to give talks about President Lincoln when requested.

Over the years that I have researched and studied President Lincoln, I have also been blessed to accumulate an office full of Lincoln books, pamphlets, statues, busts, pictures, and other valuable Lincoln memorabilia. Three of my possessions are my most prized. One is an original picture of the hanging of four of the co-conspirators who planned to assassinate our 16th President. (Purchased for $.75 in a Dallas, Texas Flea Market). Another valued item is an exact replica (including an inscription on the inside) of the pocket watch President Lincoln was in possession of on April 14, 1865, the night he was shot in Ford's Theater by veteran actor John Wilkes Booth.

Perhaps my most valuable possession is an actual white mourning ribbon worn by people on their lapels following

Lincoln's death which reads, "OUR MARTYRED FATHER! WE MOURN HIS LOSS."

I purchased the ribbon over a Lincoln on-line auction several years ago. I also own an exact replica of the .44 derringer single shot pistol used by John Wilkes Booth to kill the President.

Studying, researching, and sharing my knowledge of our 16th President has been one of the most meaningful accomplishments of my life. President Lincoln's legacy only continues to grow and impact hundreds of new lives favorably every year despite President Lincoln having less than one year of formal education.

CHAPTER 17

"Retirement"

In the latter part of 2018, I began to discuss retirement with Marvel and with Judy Buck, our office manager. I had been a lawyer for 60 years and had enjoyed the career choice that I had made many years previous.

I was confronted with the fact that my memory and thinking powers had begun to falter at times. For most jobs that would be very serious, but with a lawyer that is the beginning of the end.

The last few months of 2018 found me working on wrapping up unfinished business and planning of retirement issues. Among those concerns were selling my half of the law-firm (real estate and business equipment, furniture, etc.) to Joshua McMahon and Scott McClelland, who, along with long-time associate, Jeffrey Lowry, wanted to continue the practice of law at 201 N. Buckeye Street, Kokomo, Indiana.

By the end of December 2018, we came up with a written understanding of how that was going to take place. The other three men and I made a deliberate effort to make a smooth transition in the firm that had been at the same location for 52 years.

Our faithful office manager for 41 years, Judy Buck, also decided this would be the right time for her to retire as well.

An unusual thing happened on the way to retirement. On Saturday, January 5, 2019, Marvel and I went to Kroger's on the south side of Kokomo. While she was in the store grocery shopping, I waited in our car outside. After about 25 minutes, she called me and said I needed to come inside the store. She didn't explain.

As I approached the checkout line, I saw Marvel being attended by a couple of Kroger employees. She had collapsed in the store and the employees placed her into a wheelchair to assist me to get her to the car.

On the way home, Marvel became very nauseated and needed assistance to get into our home. As I helped her into our bathroom just off our kitchen, she collapsed and slumped to the floor. I attempted to talk to her and received no response. When I moved my hands in front of her eyes, her eyes did not flinch. I knew I had no choice but to call 911. Within five to seven minutes, the Harrison Township fire department arrived and placed my unresponsive wife on a stretcher. After checking her vitals, the men took her to the ER of Ascension St. Vincent Hospital, on the west side of Kokomo. I followed in my car.

It was determined by the ER doctor that Marvel had sustained a ruptured bowel and performed emergency surgery at 3:00 am on Sunday morning, January 6, 2019. Doctor Shadi Aboudi explained that he had tied up the bowel temporarily, but she would need more surgery in a couple of days. I called Kevin, Linda, and Jeff to make them aware of Marvel's condition and medical challenges.

Kevin drove down to Kokomo from Detroit the following day. We could be with her in intensive care for two or three more days before a second surgery was performed on Wednesday morning, January 9. Dr. Aboudi came to me in the intensive care waiting room and explained that we had to make an important decision; try to reconnect the severed bowel or to give her a permanent colostomy. I asked the doctor what he would recommend if Marvel was his mother or wife.

Because of her age, 84, and weak immune system, without hesitation he said, "permanent colostomy." I responded, "Give her the colostomy." He performed the permanent surgery.

Linda arrived in town on Wednesday afternoon and Kevin returned to his home in Detroit, Michigan.

For the next two weeks, Linda and I spent most of our days with Marvel in intensive care. Marvel now states that she has no memory of the two surgeries and the two weeks stay in intensive care.

The word of Marvel's medical challenge and her need of prayer soon spread across the country and to friends literally around the world. The medical team at the hospital told me that if I had waited another 30 minutes to call 911, Marvel would no longer be with us. Prayers were offered up to heaven on Marvel's behalf from many family members and friends and Marvel was moved from intensive care to the general population of the hospital two weeks following the second surgery.

As she continued to make progress, Marvel was eventually moved to Wellbrooke rehabilitation center on the southwest side of Kokomo. Following the recuperation stint at Wellbrooke, she returned home 54 days after her January 5, traumatic visit to the hospital. Marvel's doctor stated that she had made a remarkable recovery.

Life would never be the same again. Over the next several months, we learned how to live with the permanent colostomy. The visiting nurses and physical therapists spent the next several months helping us to adapt to a new lifestyle, namely, living with a permanent colostomy with all of its unpredictable nuances.

Marvel has been a real trouper adjusting to a whole new lifestyle. She has never complained or become bitter about her new life with this permanent change.

God's timing is always perfect. I retired from law on December 31, 2018. Marvel's life changing event happened five days later. Our plans to spend three months in Florida in 2019 were postponed for a year.

People often ask, "How do you like retirement from the practice of law?" I reply jokingly, "I don't know as I now have a new career in nursing care."

Back to retirement, Marvel and I did spend the first three months of 2020 in Punta Gorda, Florida at our daughter and son-in-law's home. In addition to relaxing and spending time with five of our great grandchildren living about two miles from our address in Florida, I did cut out time to work on the book you are reading right now.

CHAPTER 18

"David Wesley Myland"

My wife, Marvel Mae (Myland) Butcher has an amazing background and heritage. Her father, David Wesley Myland, was born in Toronto, Canada in 1858. To put that date in perspective, Abraham Lincoln was assassinated in 1865. After moving to the United States at an early age, D.W. Myland embarked on an incredible journey in the service of his Lord Jesus Christ.

Over the rest of his life, David W. Myland was used by God as a pastor, evangelist, author, poet, musician, and song writer and was also instrumental in founding two Bible colleges, one in Plainfield, Indiana and one in Chicago, Illinois.

Marvel's father was a contemporary of several giants of the Christian faith such as Dwight L. Moody, A.B. Simpson, and Oswald J. Smith. Father Myland was also involved in the founding of the Christian and Missionary Alliance movement and the Assemblies of God denomination.

Marvel has many of her father's gospel song books which contain many songs he wrote. One of the song books contains a song co-written by her father and D.L. Moody. She also possesses many beautiful poems written by her father over his lifetime.

Perhaps the most prized possession is her father's preaching Bible which she has given to our son, James Kevin Butcher, who has been a pastor since 1983.

Marvel's father married her mother rather late in his life. Marvel's mother, Lela Mae was 27 years old when Marvel was born in Columbus, Ohio. Her father was 77 years of age when God brought Marvel into David and Lela's family. Reverend Myland said, in observing his new daughter, "Now, this is a Marvel," There, her name was chosen.

Being born to Christian parents who were involved in various ministries, Marvel accepted Jesus Christ as her Savior at the age of ten. She prayed to receive Christ in the presence of Ruth Zeimer, a Christian and Missionary Alliance missionary to the Philippine Islands.

Marvel's mother, Lela Mae Myland, was a gifted pianist and actually played the piano for the well-known lady evangelist of the early 1920's, Aimee Semple McPherson, in Los Angeles, California.

Largely as a result of the early prayers and Godly influences of her mother and father, as well as a Christ honoring grandmother, Marvel enrolled in Bible College in Detroit, Michigan in 1952 to prepare for a life of serving God.

It was there that God brought us together to serve Him as a couple for the rest of our lives.

I would be remiss if I also did not mention the love and encouragement Marvel received from her step-father, George Gallant, especially during her teenage years.

All the above influences on Marvel helped prepare her to be a gifted teacher of children. However, I believe her greatest ministry has been teaching adult ladies Bible studies and mentoring younger Christian women in Kokomo, Indiana for the past 30-40 years.

CHAPTER 19

"COVID-19"

During the latter part of July, 2020, I found myself sustaining several falls in our home. My first fall occurred in our large living room when my legs collapsed under me and I fell against the concrete hearth of our fireplace. That fall resulted in three cracked ribs.

A few weeks later I fell twice in our bedroom in the middle of the night. The last fall resulted in a non-operative break in my spine. Finally, I fell (while using my walker) and was taken to St. Vincent Ascension Hospital by 911 responders.

During my arrival at the emergency room of the hospital, I was diagnosed as having Covid-19. Apparently, my symptoms included fever, a touch of pneumonia, loss of taste, and much confusion. Seven nights and eight days later, I was released and sent back home.

I have no idea where I picked up the virus. When I was out in public (which was very rare in the preceding months), I wore a mask and even gloves on some occasions.

Marvel and I were very pleased that she did not get the virus as her immune system is very weak. Fortunately, I responded well to the treatment I received and came home to be quarantined for another week. While recuperating at home from the hospital stay, I sustained some additional falls, none of which required a 911 call or additional medical assistance.

I do not remember the first three days in the hospital, but during the recovery period several things impressed me.

First, I learned how quickly you can go from a normal time in your life to a very serious (and often fatal) illness.

Second, I was reminded how blessed we are in America to have wonderful hospitals and qualified medical personnel to meet emergency needs of our citizens.

Third, I was reminded how many caring friends and neighbors that we have who called, sent cards and letters, shopped for groceries, prepared meals, cleaned our home, etc. and generally showed their love and concern for Marvel and me. I particularly want to mention Kim and Jeff Weed and Jane Eaton who went above and beyond in their concern and care. I know we had family members and friends from around the world who were praying for God to intervene and heal. Their prayers were heard and answered.

CHAPTER 20

"A Lasting Legacy"

I have written this book to share how God has guided every step of my life and, despite my many mistakes, has blessed me and my family in abundant ways.

If I had an opportunity to start life all over again, I cannot think of any major decisions I would change. God has known my innermost thoughts and motivations to accomplish what He has allowed me to do.

I trust and pray that my life has been influential in pointing not only members of my immediate family, but people I have never met personally, to see the wisdom and rewards of living their lives centered on the LORD JESUS CHRIST and HIS WORD.

The hours of prayer offered to Almighty God on behalf of myself, and my soul-mate, Marvel, by our parents and grandparents many years ago, have certainly been answered.

Their humble beginnings and lifestyles would not cause the casual observer to assess their lives as being productive and rewarding. However, they understood the importance of instilling biblical values early in their children's lives. They also, by their life styles, set Godly examples of how to live life to the fullest here on earth and prepare for spending eternity with God.

As I mentioned in Chapter five, our three children accepted Jesus Christ as their Lord and Savior early in their lives.

Kevin, our oldest, went to Taylor University in Upland, Indiana, and obtained a Bachelor of Arts degree in psychology in the spring of 1976. He received his Master of Theology Degree from Dallas Theological Seminary in Dallas, Texas in 1983. His senior thesis was about the life of Dr. David Wesley Myland, his grandfather. It's now required reading by all Dallas Theological Seminary students who major in church history.

Kevin and his wife, Carla (Stump) Butcher, whom he met at Taylor University, have pastored three churches. The first was Grace Baptist Church in Montpelier, Indiana for four years. He then served as the Senior Pastor at Grace Community Church in Detroit, Michigan (formally Ebeneezer Baptist Church) for approximately fourteen years and finally Kevin and Carla served at Hope Community Church (which they helped to found) located on East Jefferson Avenue in the Jefferson Chalmers neighborhood of Detroit for fifteen years.

Kevin has followed his God-given passion to bring the good news of Jesus Christ to people of all races and socio-economic backgrounds. Pastor Butcher has spoken all over the United States and various foreign countries during the past several years. More recently he founded Rooted Ministries Inc., a 501-C-3 entity, a much-needed ministry to pastors and other church leaders who need to be loved, appreciated, encouraged, and motivated to keep on sharing the love of Jesus with their constituents. Kevin has convinced me that some pastors are the loneliest people in the world.

In 2016, Kevin authored his first book, "Choose and Choose Again; The Brave Act of Returning to God's Love", (Nav Press/Tyndale, 2016) which sold over 10,000 copies in its initial printing. Kevin's second book "Free: Rescued from Shame-Based Religion into the Life-Giving Love of Jesus" (NavPress/Tyndale) was released April 6, 2021. Carla, a lover of children, taught elementary school for three years in Dallas, Texas, took time off to be a full-time mom, and then was a well-respected ESL (English as a second language) teacher for the last 16 years of her career in the Grosse Pointe, Michigan public school system.

Kevin and Carla have been blessed with three daughters; namely Andrea Jeanne, Leigh Anne, and Caroline Elizabeth. Andrea and Leigh Anne have both graduated from Taylor University and Caroline graduated from Eastern University in Philadelphia, Pennsylvania.

Andrea married Dusty DiSanto whom she met while attending Taylor. They now live in Highlands Ranch, Colorado where they are parents to four children: Ada Jeanne, Mack William, Van James and Dottie Annelizabeth. Dusty is on staff at Denver Seminary, in Denver, Colorado.

Leigh Anne is married to John Alexander Hague. Both hold Masters Degrees in counseling and are licensed professional Christian Counselors in the Denver, Colorado area. Two children, Johnny VI and Lennie Lou.

Finally, Kevin and Carla's youngest daughter, Caroline Elizabeth is living in Boulder, Colorado and is in pursuit of a Master's degree in Fine Arts, with an emphasis in dance at the University of Colorado, Boulder.

Linda Michelle Long is our middle child and our only daughter. Linda and her husband, Norm Long, also met at Taylor University in Upland, Indiana in the mid 1970's. They have been married for 43 plus years.

Norm and Linda are both retired public school teachers and live in Needham, Indiana just a few miles southeast of Indianapolis, Indiana. However, they spend much of their time ministering to other people, assisting them in facing challenges of daily living in a fallen world. They show their acts of love and kindness from a Biblical perspective which many people struggle to understand and apply to their lives. They are also deeply involved in a Missionary Ministry in the country of Liberia in church planting.

The Longs were blessed with two children, Neil Robert Long and Allison Michelle (Long) Laman. Neil met his wife, Erin Kingma at Taylor University. The Longs live in Denver, Colorado, where Neil is the executive pastor at Park Church. Erin works part-time from home. They have been blessed with two sons, Everett James, and Asher Brooks.

Allison also met her future husband, Michael Laman, at Taylor University where both were students. The Lamans have six young children and live in Punta Gorda, Florida. They maintain a Christian home and homeschool their children: Shiloh Peace, Evangeline Grace, Judah Courage, Gabriel Shepherd, Eden Promise, and Isaiah Arrow. Mike and Allison both have a love for music and spend their spare time writing and composing Christian songs.

Our youngest son, Jeffrey Kent Butcher, was born in Kokomo, Indiana in 1960. Jeff married Paula Ricci, whom he met while both attended Kokomo, Indiana high school. Jeff was a teacher and coach at Franklin Central Middle School in southeastern Marion County, Indiana. Paula was a second grade teacher at Center Grove Elementary School in Greenwood, Indiana. They moved to the State of Washington a few years ago and are very active in their church in Bellingham, Washington. Jeff served many years on the deacon board of Immanuel Church in Greenwood, Indiana, many of them as chairman. He also taught different Bible classes on varying subjects. Paula and Jeff are both involved in small group ministries as well. Jeff and Paula have two children, Nathan James Butcher and Leah Christine Butcher. Both children went to Taylor University and married people whom they met at this Christian college.

Nathan is married to Theresa Westra and they have three children; Theodore James, Lucy Beth, and Oliver Jonathan. Nathan and Theresa and family reside in Bellingham, Washington where he is a realtor and Theresa is involved in public relations at the realty firm. The younger Butchers are very involved in their church as well, with the young people and music.

Leah Christine (Butcher) Parker is married to Cameron Parker, whom she met as a student at Taylor University. The Parkers have two sons, Jack Francis Parker and Milo Wynn Parker. They reside in the Ferndale, Washington area. Leah works at the real estate firm where her brother, Nathan, is a realtor. Cam works as a graphic designer. They thoroughly enjoy the beauty and intrigue of the northwest with their two young sons.

Marvel and I have attempted to invest into the lives of our individual family members which includes our children, their spouses, our grandchildren, and their spouses, and our great grandchildren.

We believe the spiritual legacy we are leaving to them is more valuable for eternity's sake than financial and monetary bequests. From all indications, it appears our legacy will be handed down to future generations until the Lord returns. *NOTHING would please us more.*

CHAPTER 21

Epilogue

*M*arvel and I are grateful that you have taken the time to read about our journey. We trust that our life experiences have been an encouragement to you and those you love.

While we made many mistakes and wrong choices in our lives, God always knew that the motives of our hearts were to honor and please our Lord Jesus Christ.

You may be reading this book 10, 20, or 50 years from now. I have no idea what your life has been like. I will never know your joys and deep sorrows that you are facing. But I can say with assurance, you are deeply loved by a God who sent His son, Jesus, to the cross for you. It may not feel like it at times. There is so much pain and mystery in life. So much that we go through that has no quick easy resolution or explanation. But, somehow in the face of Jesus of Nazareth, we see a sacrificial love—for all of us, that gives hope in the storm. If you are struggling, I can understand why you would want to run as fast as you can from religion—even some forms of Christianity. But, let me encourage you—Jesus isn't a religion. He's the One who loves you with all of His heart and desires to be an integral part of your life. He is the one who never fails or disappoints. He is the one who is always there when needed. I encourage you to invite Him into your life. He waits with open arms.

May God bless you richly as you continue your journey with HIM.

START YOUR NEW LIFE
WITH CHRIST

You can have real, lasting peace today through a relationship with Jesus Christ. Start your four-step journey now!

STEP 1- God loves you and has a plan for you! The Bible says, "God so loved the world that He gave His one and only Son, (Jesus Christ), that whoever believes in Him shall not perish, but have eternal life" (John 3:16).

Jesus said, "I came that they may have life and have it abundantly"- a complete life full of purpose (John 10:10).

But here's the problem:

STEP 2- People are sinful and separated from God.

We have all done, thought, or said bad things, which the Bible calls "sin." The Bible says, "All have sinned and fall short of the glory of God" (Romans 3:23).

The result of sin is death, spiritual separation from God (Romans 6:23).

The Good News?

STEP 3- God sent His Son to die for your sins!

Jesus died in our place so we could have a relationship with God and be with Him forever.

"God demonstrates His own love toward us, in that while we were yet sinners, Christ died for us" (Romans 5:8).

But it didn't end with His death on the cross. He rose again and still lives!

"Christ died for our sins ... He was buried ... He was raised on the third day, according to the Scriptures"

(1 Corinthians 15:3,4).

Jesus is the only way to God, Jesus said, "I am the way, the truth, and the life; no one comes to the Father, but through Me" (John 14:6).

STEP 4- Would you like to receive God's forgiveness?

We can't earn salvation; we are saved by God's grace when we have faith in His Son, Jesus Christ. All you have to do is believe you are a sinner, that Christ died for your sins, and ask forgiveness. Then turn from your sins – that's called repentance. Jesus Christ knows you and loves you. What matters to Him is the attitude of your heart, your honesty. We suggest praying the following prayer to accept Christ as your Savior:

"Dear God, I know I'm a sinner, and I ask for your forgiveness. I believe Jesus Christ is your Son. I believe that He died for my sin and that you raised Him to life. I want to trust Him as my Savior and follow Him as Lord, from this day forward. Guide my life and help me to do your will. I pray this in the name of Jesus. Amen."

Printed in the United States
by Baker & Taylor Publisher Services